TALES
OF A
JAILHOUSE
LIBRARIAN

CHALLENGING THE
JUVENILE JUSTICE SYSTEM
ONE BOOK AT A TIME

MARYBETH ZEMAN

D1056242

VINEGAR HILL PRESS, BROOKLYN, NY

Vinegar Hill Press, Inc.
52 Fort Greene Place
Brooklyn, New York 11217
855.853 7171

ISBN 13: 978-0-6159538-7-8
LCCN: Pending

Cover design by Weiman Design, LLC
© 2013 Weiman Design

Distributed by Amazon.com and Ingram Worldwide Distribution Services

Printed in the United States of America

Dedicated to all the boys
who found their escape in books …
May they discover a new freedom and a new happiness,
and to my husband Michael,
who encouraged me to discover mine.

CONTENTS

Prologue   xiii

1   Diquan   1

2   Hector   9

3   When They Go   15

4   Our Five-Classroom Schoolhouse   19

5   David   25

6   "All the world's a stage"   31

7   Francisco   37

8   Philanthropy   43

9   Dyshone   49

10   Hurricanes and Other Disasters   57

11   Kourtney and the Boys in Classroom 4   63

12   Dawuan   71

13   "I swear to tell the truth…the whole truth"   77

14   *The Shawshank Redemption*   *81*

15   Rodolfo   85

16   Lockdowns   91

17	Kris	97
18	No Visitors Today	103
19	David's Secret	111
20	Rasheed and Isaiah	119
21	Ishmel Is Free to Read	123
22	Tyshana	127
23	Angelo	131
24	Invictus	137
25	Freddy	143
26	Kris and Elliot	149
27	Dante	155
28	Graduation—Pizza, a Handshake, and a Bottle of Coke	161
29	Damion	167
30	Laquan	171
31	Ishmel's Transparency	179
32	Choices	185
33	Nausan	189
34	Aidan	199
35	Maurice	205

CONTENTS

36	Innocent Until Proven Guilty	211
37	Kris Goes Up Top	217
38	David's Dreads	221
39	Jacquell	227
40	Jacquell's Father	231
41	Laquan Is Found	235
42	Night School	243
43	Tyshana's Son	249
44	Addy	253
45	Mary, The Lady from the Library	259
46	Derek	265
47	Reaching Out	271
48	David, Barney, and Wesley	277
49	Hector's Gift	283
50	Hope Whispers	289
51	Sister Dolores	295
52	Boys with Blank Pages	301
The Facts		305
Resources		309

Acknowledgments   323

About the Author   325

Endnotes   327

"It is said that no one truly knows a nation until one has been inside its jails. A nation should not be judged by how it treats its highest citizens, but its lowest ones."

—Nelson Mandela

Prologue

You always wonder how you end up in jail.

I know I did.

I'd been a high school teacher for close to thirty years. Mostly, ESL (English as a second language). Every day, I walked into the same quintessential 1950s, sprawling brick building. There was always the same American flag perched atop the flagpole and the same crackly morning announcements followed by the Pledge of Allegiance. Bright September's autumn sun, cold and dark December mornings, and the reassuring light of spring's return. And yes, teenage energy. Blackboards. Chalk. Computers. Slamming locker doors. The lingering scent of Jessica Simpson or Britney Spears, or whatever pop star cologne was in. Braces. Gym classes running round the track. Marching band practices, marching across the field. Bells. Always bells that began and ended every single event of the day.

Unlike most people, I hadn't been sentenced here. I volunteered.

Now, each morning, there is the endless maze of gates that begins my day. My movement dictated by a guard, not a bell. And my entry into a colorless cinder block world. There are few windows here—all, lonely, metal slatted, jalousie, intentionally restricting light. Most covered with pigeon droppings. There is nothing here to wake up to but a windowless and dark cell. The faint cooing of pigeons nesting outside signals break of day.

There is no dawn. There is a staleness to even the beginning of day. A lifelessness you can smell. There is so little air. The smell of the mustiest of basements. Or the moist, thick air of a Louisiana swamp absent the heat. It is continually chilly. In winter, no heat. In summer, the artificial arctic air blasts from dripping air conditioning vents. There is so little air. None of it real. You smell the mold. You smell it, and then you see it forming its washed charcoal on the stucco wall in the yard. As if there had once been a mural there. The faces on it washed away as quickly as the faces of the inmates pass, boarding the buses to the courts. There is the same American flag perched atop a flagpole outside; but there is no pledge, no allegiance to anything. September to December to April to June— it is all the same. Dark. A palpable darkness. A perpetual staleness. A shared human lethargy. I miss the morning lockers slamming and homeroom chatter as I walk the long voiceless hallways here. I hear only footsteps. Mine.

And jail was my escape.

An overbearing principal. My second husband, seriously ill, mounting hospital bills—*How could I be going through this again?* The thought of spending my last years teaching thirteen-year-olds—a horrible age no matter which side of it you're on. The housing market had collapsed like a Florida sinkhole, with our home in it. My youngest sister's battle with kidney cancer (the same damning disease that took my first husband, John). And now my husband Michael—confined to a hospital bed, infections invading his body without defense.

All reasons to escape. Jail seemed perfect for me.

And I did. Escape. Well, changed positions would be a more accurate and professional way of putting it—ESL teacher to transitional counselor. A huge jump. Transitional counselor, helping students move from jail back to school or work or home. Helping them smooth the ride.

But I was the one making the transition; I was having enough trouble negotiating my own; I had no idea how I was going to help anyone with his.

I was quite familiar with transitions. In fact, I almost hated the word. Wasn't it just a synonym for life? Having to put up with whatever punches life dealt you.

On the surface, I had the credentials for the job. On the surface, I looked good. (I "presented well.") On the surface, I'd work more hours and get more pay. On the surface, my principal would be left behind. On the surface, I wouldn't be facing thirteen-year-olds. This was the job for me.

Looking back, I'd like to say that I recognized some Mother Teresa-like motivation lurking somewhere underneath it all. That I felt some need for frequent flyer canonization points. I didn't. I was just planning an escape. I just never imagined where exactly I was escaping to. Or what I might find.

Beneath the surface, things were percolating though. Thoughts that were making me think I might actually be perfect for this job. That I had something that might count. Something that could make a difference. There were things you couldn't see. Things that you don't put on your resume. I could be a helluva transitional counselor—if I could only figure it out.

Transitions. Those bumps in the roads. Those times when life gets you by the throat, and you want to yell, "I give up," and you don't—and it finally loosens its hold. I don't have to explain it. If you've ever been that close to life strangling you and struggling for breath, you know what that first exhilarating gasp of air feels like. You thank God, catch your breath, and move on. A transition.

They're painful. But they change you. They leave you with something to give back that nothing else can. Life experience.

I had lots of it.

Mother. Widow. Three troubled and grieving kids. Another marriage. Lots of my own therapy. Not one but two seriously ill husbands. One dead. The other hanging on for life. Too much grief.

I had a new job to do, and I didn't have a clue.

I had left a high school full of cheerleaders and pep rallies and yearbook photos and entered into a world filled with unkempt boys dressed in orange uniforms and assigned long numbers alongside their names.

I knew how to teach English; I knew how to teach social studies; I knew how to teach students to write, but I didn't know how to help students cope with jail, or fear, or life—all real subjects here.

Troubled boys. With really desperate needs. I understood their chaos, and pain, and confusion. I had lived some of it. Life experience. I had lots of it. So did they. That's all I had to give.

I was as desperate to survive as they. And I was smart enough not to show it. My instinct told me that fear was not admired here. In the beginning, that was my focus—how do I survive? It's what you do when you first come in.

And I begin.

I listen.

There's so much to be learned from listening.

It is timeless. Universal. A basic human need. To be heard.

"Out of the depths have I cried unto thee, O Lord..." The desperate plea to be heard.

We listen to the anguish. We understand. We offer comfort.

I listen, too. It's the only thing I know how to do. And it's such a simple action.

Then I realize—I'm not trying to escape. I'm more interested in helping these boys escape. I want them to escape—one more failure, one more trip to jail, one more arrest. I want them to be freed.

One of my students asks for a book. Then another one. They complain of being bored and having nothing else to do. I listen to student after student, boy by boy, tell me about the books they like or wish they could read while they are stuck in their cells. While they are stuck in the most boring place on the planet. Those books spoke volumes about them.

But those books spoke volumes to me. When I listened. They reminded me of my passion for books, which had prompted my going to school only four years before. That my masters in library science, tucked in a drawer, unused because of the economy and a shortage of jobs, didn't have to be reserved for a so-called second career, now deferred.

Life experience.

I started to get the books they loved. And they started to read them. And I figured out a way to do my counseling. Well, to make the connection, I needed to counsel.

Call it grace. Once I did, it became so simple.

The inscription over the library at Thebes: Medicine for the Soul.

We all understand it as a place of escape. Each and every book, an opportunity for escape.

Freedom. Escape. Healing for the soul.

To be freed from the boredom and tedium that are an inmate's daily companion.

To be healed. To be comforted. To be inspired.

A lot of the time, I wonder how I ended up in jail—just as my students do. A lot of them tell me they know God had a reason. This is a tough place for God to put a seventeen-year-old. But I know God had a reason for putting me here. Pure grace. To let me see just how big hope can be when it rekindles its flame.

My title: transitional counselor.

My blessing: jailhouse librarian.

"Blessed are those who mourn …"
—Matthew 5:4

Chapter 1

Diquan

Jails and libraries have little in common save one thing: they both have rigid standards of classification and cataloging. With libraries, there's one system. One way to add new things to a collection. One way to do things. Or there'd be total chaos. Total disorganization and disarray.

Jails, too, subscribe to the same rigid standards. There are rules. There are regulations. And there's only one way to do things. The way it's always been done, and more than likely, it will always be done. Without it, total chaos. Total disarray.

It's difficult though when there are fault lines that erupt beneath those standards. When you fall in between the cracks.

Diquan rarely asked to see me. When he did, it was for pesky little things—pens, pencils, or to check a court date—nothing too intense. In fact, that's how I might describe Diquan—not too intense. Small, wiry, curly soft black hair. There was nothing tough about him. He was an agreeable kid. So many of our students are—agreeable. You'd wonder how they did disagreeable things.

Diquan's teacher, Mrs. K, not Diquan, called out to me as I walked past her classroom door.

"Mrs. Z, do you think you'd have time to see Diquan, this morning? He'd like to speak with you."

I'd make a point to. Kids who rarely asked to be seen usually had good reason to when they did ask. I didn't hesitate to answer. Or want him to have to wait too long. "I'll be back in two."

Diquan smiled a somewhat more than mellow smile.

When we finally sat down, I soon found out why. Diquan's brother had been killed—shot. Yet another gang murder. Too many of them. Another victim of the streets. A name not even printed in the newspaper. He was only sixteen, but in Hempstead, not newsworthy. Just dead.

"I am so sorry, Diquan." What else could be said?

We sat in silence for a moment. Diquan needed comfort. Solace. I knew he needed more than I could give.

We both sat with a painful helplessness. It was he who was brave enough to punch through the shroud of sadness now hung in the room.

"Mrs. Z, do you think I'd be able to go home for the funeral?"

"It would be good if you could, Diquan." I acknowledged both of our concerns. "I think you put a request through the chaplain's office."

"Yeah, when my mom called, they sent some priest or something to tell me about my brother, but I haven't talked to him since."

There were several chaplains—a "priest or something," as Diquan called him: a Muslim imam whose call to prayer

2

filled our school hallways on Friday afternoons, and a Jewish rabbi who came on Monday nights and celebrated a Passover breakfast instead of Seder, and the Episcopalian minister, Larry, who probably marched alongside me in 1970 in Washington, D.C. And then there were the two Catholic nuns, sans habits, looking very much like older versions of Susan Sarandon. There was the oddly austere Baptist minister who arrived without a lively choir, and a Catholic deacon from Puerto Rico. This odd assortment was called our prison ministry, and I really didn't care which one of them showed up. I don't think Diquan cared either. I just wanted him to talk to someone who cared, cared enough to get him home—by Monday.

But in the here and now, I cared about what was happening to him. His sixteen-year-old brother was dead. The only reason Diquan had outlived him—he was in jail. How cruel the streets really were.

"I'll talk to the chaplain as soon as I can," I told him. "Have you been able to talk to your mother?"

"Once. She don't have minutes left on my account, and she can't put no more money on her card. And she's busy making funeral plans and stuff."

Diquan's account wouldn't be the first to go dead. Crime and jail and phones are punishment and business. Just like funerals. Now Diquan's mom was worrying about the money she had to spend on her other son.

But here and now, I was worried about the son who was still alive.

"How are you taking care of yourself, Diquan? Losing a brother is a big thing. It's really hard not to be able to say good-bye."

3

He shrugged off my concern as easily as if he had just walked into a spider web and was brushing off its sticky remnants.

"Are you talking to anyone? Did that priest come back to see you again?"

He shook his head.

"Do you know Sister Dolores? The sister who worked with you on math?"

He looked at me blankly. He wouldn't have identified that nice older woman in the hallway as anyone other than the lady who had helped him with math. He didn't see anything "sisterly" about her.

"I'm going to talk to Sister Dolores and ask her to find out if you can go home for the funeral. Let's see what she can do."

He smiled. Such a trusting smile. As if he was sure I was going to accomplish everything he asked. I wasn't sure I was going to accomplish anything.

It wasn't against the rules for an inmate to attend a relative's wake. It just wasn't easy. The jail runs like a well-organized machine. Any movement, even one inmate's, impedes the machine. So, rules or no rules, it wasn't easy calibrating the machine differently.

Attending a wake and participating in a family's grief are two different things. Inmates view the body alone. Without the comfort of other family members. Without participating in the service.

Adding more sorrow to the home-going service Diquan's mother was trying to plan, he'd still be dressed in orange, shackled and cuffed—his only comfort, the guards who accompanied him. But able to say his good-bye. It was all about being able to say good-bye. And I hoped Diquan would be able to say his.

C. S. Lewis acknowledged that the death of someone you love is like an amputation. I took great consolation in his book on grief when I had to deal with the loss of my own loved ones. But a book only offers words to weep with. Grief is not to be suffered alone. Our sorrow begs for someone to weep with.

I ran around the hall to the chaplains' offices, hoping to catch one of them there and found Larry, our Episcopalian minister. I knew he'd do what he could do.

The next morning, I saw a brighter, more hopeful Diquan. Larry had stopped to see him. They were trying to make arrangements to have him go home.

Sister Dolores called Diquan out into the hall and talked with him, and it wasn't just to help with math.

It seemed like everything was a go. The sergeant was on it; transportation was involved. The well-oiled machine was slowing down just a bit, giving Diquan time to get off and get on again.

When I left work, I said a prayer.

When I came back, I had to say several more.

Walking by classroom 3, I poked my head in the door. "How'd everything go, Diquan?"

"I didn't go." There was no anger, no regret—only resignation. A boy used to disappointment. And sensing a need to comfort me, he added, "It's okay."

But it wasn't okay.

"Why don't you come across the hall, and we'll talk?" We walked across to my desk and chair.

"What happened? You were all set to go."

Diquan shrugged. "My mom couldn't give them anything quick enough with my brother's name and mine on it to prove that we were brothers. We don't have the same last names."

The rules. The regulations. Proving who's your relative and who's not. Not just your mother's word. Falling between the cracks.

"I'm so sorry, Diquan. It was important for you to say good-bye."

We talked about his brother a little. What they liked to do. The kind of movies they watched. Something stupid he said. And then I suggested he write him a letter.

"It's only a suggestion, but sometimes it helps people to put into words what they might have said when they can't say good-bye in person. I think it will help you feel better."

I brought Diquan a notebook and a pen and thought of the many people I said good-bye to in my lifetime. I thought of my husband John, whom I had buried so many years ago. I thought of my present husband Michael, lying in the hospital bed at Methodist Hospital. And my sister Irene, who was still battling with her cancer for six years. We're never prepared to say our good-byes, but Diquan and his brother had never once thought of theirs. They were too young to think about good-bye. I was old enough to know better.

"Blessed are those who mourn, for they shall be comforted." Matthew 5:4

"We are all prisoners, but some of us are in cells with windows and some without."
—Kahlil Gibran

Chapter 2

Hector

Hector faced the death penalty a couple of months ago, but his execution was not likely in New York State. In 2008 then-Governor David Paterson issued an executive order requiring the removal of all execution equipment from all New York State facilities. The death penalty here hadn't been abolished—it was on hold, but Hector at least knew that, right now, there's nobody sitting on death row and no electric chairs waiting to be plugged in.

Hector can rest assured that he won't be dying by lethal injection while he's sitting in our county jail. Right now.

But he's in on very serious charges—and federal charges at that. In the federal system, gang conspiracy, gang murder, even as muddled as figuring out who did what and who didn't, can still render a death sentence. But they're rare—only three since 1963, and all by lethal injection.

About a month ago, Hector was relieved to find out he was only facing a life sentence without parole. Kind of tough dealing with nineteen-year-olds who are relieved at the prospect of spending the rest of their lives in prison.

Not knowing the exact actuarial figures, I'd estimate

that'd be about sixty-something years in jail—not much of a life. At least to me.

On the outside, Hector broke all the rules—gang involvement, gang assault, gang conspiracy, and worse of all, from what I gather, gang murder. Federal offenses ... federal time. But Hector's not alone. More than half of the people—50.3 percent—convicted for federal felonies since 2011 were Latino. I know the rules. I am certainly not condoning anyone who has broken them so egregiously. I do know though that Hector didn't sign up for the MS-13 gang as my sons did for Cub Scouts. He hadn't even been given that choice. My sons' friends joined Cub Scouts, Little League, and altar boys. And my two boys still got in some trouble after my husband died. They were adolescents, and life and adolescence don't often equal tranquility. For Hector, like many Latino boys, members of their family, their friends, or their acquaintances were in gangs first. Instead of Cub Scouts. And like many Latino boys, interestingly not the girls, only 58 percent graduate from high school. For those, like Hector, who drop out, who are hanging out on the street with little to do, and who aren't getting a decent job, a gang means survival more than a club membership.

For the most part, I avoid finding out about the charges. I don't want to know what Hector's done. I deal with the person in front of me, not the person he left behind. Here, I see a totally different person. I see a glimpse of the person Hector might have been before the gangs, before the crimes, before the police, and before his arrest.

I see the Hector who migrated here with his parents from El Salvador. I see the Hector who struggled to learn

English and to do well in school. The Hector whose parents couldn't help him with homework. The Hector who was left at home alone while his parents worked two and three jobs. I see a family who never dreamed of their son spending his life in the United States in jail. They had worked toward the American dream, while Hector destroyed his own.

This isn't like the other jobs I've had in schools. I don't have conferences to meet parents. I don't speak with the teachers he had before. I have the Hector here and now. Maybe for an instant. Maybe a couple of months. The question always persists: *What difference can I make?*

Here, Hector follows a lot of the rules now. He is the best personal assistant I have. He returns all the books he borrows. He can't get his hands on enough books to read. Hector is beginning to frame out his life in prison in the books he reads, and he is beginning to reframe the young man he is. I see little changes in him. That tough exterior softens in Mrs. P's classroom. He's working one on one with her and feeling confident about his academic progress. He wants to pass his GED. He actually thinks that would be an accomplishment. He doesn't just ask for the mysteries or graphic novels anymore. Or the books in Spanish. I can tell he's feeling more at ease with reading books in English, and his book selections are becoming more varied. I can't help wondering: *if* he had read books outside of jail, would his life have been different? I keep wondering why his life couldn't have been different.

Hector's been in Ad Seg, in a segregated population lately, and not in school, so the only academics he's been receiving is through the books we've sent back and forth. He's been put in what's commonly known as solitary confinement. So it's a kind of censored reading list he's been receiving without protest. I passed along a book, *The Barrio Kings*, a rather provocative title, one that might heighten the scrutiny of a CO or two, but proved to get Hector's attention.

We don't know how much longer he'll be with us in the county jail before being transferred to the federal penitentiary, so he wrote his teacher a note this week. He's been reading the Bible—yes, jail is definitely an evangelical moment. But, maybe just as importantly, he read *The Barrio Kings* and thought about the character, José, who managed to escape the gang and go on to lead a life without them. Hector thought about his choices and thought about his future in a prison life with or without much the same thing. Odds are, it will be very tough to move on to life in prison without gang support, but Hector thought about the possibility. It made me think about the power of books and encouraged me to keep pushing that cart.

"Books Are For Use—chained books cannot migrate ...
past the length of their chain."
—S.R. Ranganathan, *The Five Laws of Library Science*

Chapter 3

When they go ...

I like Hector. He is bright, thoughtful, and holds amazing promise. I see it and realize how limited his potential is. It is one of the hard realities that is sinking in about this job.

I expected some of it. The dark cinder block building. I just didn't realize how dark it was. The rules. I just didn't realize how many there were. I never realized the sense of loss that seeps through every air molecule and every inch of space. Its sadness. I never realized how little happiness there could be here.

I think of all the years of education I have. My degrees. Sure, I can teach. I can help students transition somewhere—if budget cuts leave any programs for them to go out to. With the Hectors, I feel less confident. For the boys sentenced to lives in just one more prison, I feel helpless. Young, barely bearded faces aging without the benefit of life. They've been weathered and beaten by life experience already. But academic degrees can't infuse the happiness missing here. I wonder what can. I'm at a loss to find it.

Hector's newfound love of reading reminds me of

something I studied in library school, so far removed from this time and place. It's odd that I even remember it, let alone connect it to jail.

But I connect it to Hector—the first law of libraries. *Things of value shouldn't be locked away forever.* The basis of the principle that "books are for use." And I think of Hector's being locked away. Forever. A person of value. I think about the promise I see and how soon it will be gone. *Where will it go?* And I ask myself that same question, *How can I make a difference?*

I'll come in one morning, and Hector will just be gone. Vanished. As easily as math problems off a board. Deleted. And that will be it.

No future Facebook friend. I'll never know what is his real end. And it's like that for almost every student I have. Here for an instant. Gone the next.

The difference between my life before and now—living on the edges of humanity instead of in between. And Hector is so near the edge.

There is sadness but remarkable resilience hidden here, too. That is an amazing discovery.

Yes, Hector is destined to a life in prison. I don't know if he deserves that sentence or not. He says he was just a bystander. *America's Invisible Children: Latino Youth and the Failure of the Justice System* asserts that anti-gang laws criminalize typical teenage behavior. It is a universal axiom: Teenagers associate with other teenagers. There are so many gang arrests, I can't separate the bystanders from the members. I do know that in California, police officials only identified about 10 percent of Latino youth as being gang members, but 84 percent of Latino youth as knowing someone in a gang. That puts the odds of being a bystander pretty high when there is "stop and frisk." I begin to gain new information about things I never dreamed I'd care about. Gangs. Youth. Public policy. I don't want it to get all mixed up. I try to focus on what I thought was just a job, not the criminal justice system.

But Hector is happy to be alive. He is happy to read his books. Happiness is reduced to its simplest form here, but the human heart finds it anyway.

And it's how this job makes my life so different. It's how Hector and Diquan and the other boys make my life so different. In them I recognize the source of human happiness, which I always knew all along. That the simplest things have great value. And we should hold them dear. The people in our lives. The sunrises. The sunsets. Time.

I'm reminded of that first principle: "Books are for use"—a thing of value shouldn't be locked away forever, and I receive the answer I need to my question. I realize how much value those books can give.

It's true. My job here is very different from my job before. These boys arrive as blank slates, numbered persons whose only identity is the charges they carry. Too often, they leave without my knowing them. Too often, there is little time for connection.

I have often found great power in the brief encounters in my life. Wisdom gained from a conversation on a plane. Watching an elderly couple holding hands on the subway. How they touched my heart and impressed upon me tender thoughts of growing old. I was so grateful for the nurse's aide who so lovingly held my husband's hand when he lay in ICU.

And I begin to understand.

"I've never let my schooling interfere with my education."
—Mark Twain

Chapter 4

Our Five-Classroom Schoolhouse

"Mrs. Z—you get any new comics?" The wheels on the four-tier cart before me squeak past a classroom full of students. There are five classrooms in all. Bigger than a one-room schoolhouse, smaller than a school cafeteria.

The same jailhouse beige colors our walls; but here and there, an inspirational sign or poster tries to disguise where the boys and I really know we are—jail. "Reach for the stars—be all that you can!" A faded banner limply hangs in the archway over the gray metal desk where our two hall monitors (two correction officers) are assigned.

The E building where the school sits is one more wing of a single main building surrounded by four cross-shaped satellites. Each satellite is like a four-armed octopus with three of its tentacles reaching out aimlessly. A fourth stays docked as tenaciously as any octopus might to its prey. So the boys walk across, above, or over easily to the school every day.

As with all things in jail, their entry and exit is controlled. A darkly lit CO sits, almost as unseen as Poe's judges opening the pit, in a *Plexiglassed* bubble beside the door and pushes the open/close button permitting access. Then they enter the long hallway of classrooms called school.

As soon as they enter, they pass what I like to call the Winners Wall. I don't know if they even notice it's there at all. Beneath a carved wooden plaque with the name of our school, when the jail budget still allowed carpentry and farming and other vocational classes, is a list of former students who got their GEDs. Of course, those boys are long gone. I often wonder if they ever came back. Studies show that the higher the education, the lower the recidivism rate. Maybe that worked for those boys. I wonder if I could have them visit and share what's happened to their lives since they left—if I'd *want* them to share what's happened to their lives since they left.

To the right are five classrooms, one not used— each with a full-length glass door—in jail, everything and everyone observed. Even teachers sit like bugs under this microscope-world. To the left, the law library, and then our computer room, filled with non-Internet connected computers. Another larger classroom, my makeshift office, and at the end, the Teachers Lounge— three cubicles, two live computers, a bathroom, a sink, and a microwave.

I wheel the cart into classroom 2. Typical of any classroom. Desks neatly arranged in rows. Whiteboard. Teacher's desk. At first glance, like any other classroom in any other school anywhere.

But then you notice—the orange. The bright orange juice duplicate outfits each and every student is wearing contrasting sharply against the very beige cinder block walls.

The very beige, bulletin-board-less, no pep rally notice-less walls.

And you notice the largely very dark complexions of almost every face, the various chocolate and tan and beige skin tones—an occasional white, freckle-faced, fair-haired boy. And you notice the boys—they're all boys.

"Hey, Mrs. Z—you get any new comics in?"

The bottom shelf of the cart is full of comics, not as many as there should be. They walk faster than other things. They're passed around in the dorms, but I love things to be passed around. My rolling library is without fines. Not without loss or grief. Not without a budget. But with awareness and with a generosity born when you recognize moments of human empowerment.

"You got any Stuart Woods, Mrs. Z? How 'bout *Immortal*? Anyone bring back *Immortal*? You have number five of Harry Potter?"

They get up out of their seats and rush the cart to see what's been brought back and what's gotten legs ... like everything else here, there's little you can depend on.

My job begins. It isn't defined by state standards or the Common Core, or by any of the educational jargon that has been in vogue over the course of my thirty-year career. Applying a standard or changing a teaching approach would be easy. Here, outcomes are hazy. Objectives are fogged in like cargo ships anxious to leave port. What is most important in the two days, or maybe thirty days, or even 260 days that we have these boys?

Curiously, jails aren't meant to hold onto inmates waiting for court cases anyway. You get arraigned, they set bail, you head home, and you go back to court. Like rock stars with ankle bracelets. Or actresses who skip bail anyway. You know, "innocent until proved guilty." Well, that's what I used to think, too.

Civilians use the words interchangeably, but there is a big difference between jail and prison. A jail is a short-term stay—less than a year's sentence, or when you're awaiting trial. Prison is for longer sentences. One is run by a county; the other, the state. I keep reminding myself that I'm working in a jail when our boys are on such extended stays, sometimes as long as a year when just waiting to go to court.

Prisons are overflowing with prisoners, and jails are overflowing with inmates, and courts are overflowing with cases, so everything moves slowly. We have a lot of boys caught in the backlog.

They are usually poor, lacking the collateral to post even the most minimal bail. When you're in on a misdemeanor with $500 bail and your grandmother who has custody of your other three brothers can't come up with the money, it's not called "tough love." We don't have much diversity in our classrooms.

And always that question resounds over and over in my head, *How can I make a difference?* It is a question that has been asked by any teacher who has ever worked in our program.

But I can see that, over time, the question can become less recurrent, the answer less important. I see it on some of the more seasoned teachers' faces. I hear it in their sarcasm. When they rain on my enthusiasm.

"Why have them sign out books?" one of them scowls. "All they do is use them as bed risers." And some of that is true. Books are stacked high beneath floor-level cots. And there's nothing better to stop a mouse from entering through a small hole in your cell. But lately, some of those books are read. I keep remembering that there's more than mice chewing on J. K. Rowling.

The in and out. The court cases jammed into a system where young boys' lives founder behind a narrow ice-clogged opening of hope. I can see how easily I can get jammed along with them. Simply join in the hopelessness.

So this job is different. My students' successes aren't measured by test scores or GED results. Their success will only be measured by the choices they make when they leave here, not the successes they have while they're in here. Their success will only be measured by their own lifetimes. Their own choices. Influences from others? Books? Themselves?

And I, likely, mightn't have anything to do with it at all.

"He who opens a school door, closes a prison."
—Victor Hugo

Chapter 5

David

The great thing about reading books is that they can change where we are, and how we are, for a few minutes or even hours every day. Period. Perspective colors everything.

David wasn't borrowing books as much as racketeering them. I suspected he had some kind of business going on the side. He'd be signing books from the cart on a regular basis; and almost as regularly, his cell was being shaken down.

"Mrs. Z, you know the Green Lantern comic I signed out? I don't got it. They shook down my hut [cell]. The CO got it." He said it with such regret that I had to believe him.

David was in on some kind of robbery charge. And not for the first time. But what you see is what you got. No flimflams. No swindles. No Ponzi schemes. With David, you knew you were being pinched.

David couldn't scam you. He was too honest for that. His grin was a little too wide, his teeth a little too spaced, and a gaping empty hole filled half his smile.

If David were to run a shell game, he'd point out the pea.

There was something charming about David where probably no charm should exist. No matter how hard you might want to avoid cliché, you could only call him scrawny—tall and lean. Splintery. A childlike fragility in an adult-size criminal.

So David "lost" the books he signed out from the cart. Without my usual protest.

And he requisitioned other supplies, too. Regulation marble notebooks that were only the regulation ten pages wide, soft covered, not hard enough to hit you over the head. And he asked for lots of regulation pens. Well, stubs of pens, short, midgets to their cousin pens. Bendable like pipe cleaners and filled just enough to write a letter, or at best, two.

He would ask me every day. "I need a notebook, Mrs. Z." And the next. "I need a pen."

"What are you doing, David, eating them?" I humored him.

"No, really, Mrs. Z. I'm writing hip-hop. I need them."

I half believed him. Envisioning a Li'l Wayne. My other half—estimating his stock.

So David had lots of reasons to come to school. His business depended on it. Getting a GED probably wasn't one of them, but that'd be worth every book I ever lost.

"You have the books you signed out, David?" I asked as I rolled the cart into room 3. It was almost perfunctory now.

"Tomorrow. I'll bring 'em back tomorrow." He provided me one of his most mischievous and dastardly Snidely Whiplash smiles. We both understood those books would never reappear.

"Hey, ya hear I passed the GED, Mrs. Z?" His eyes dashed with amusement.

"I did, David. Congratulations." I handed someone a book.

"I gotta ask you a favor, Mrs. Z. Can we talk?"

Almost immediately, I prepared to get another pen from the supply cabinet as we walked across the hall to my office, classroom 5.

"I need you to get a hold of my sister, Mrs. Z. Ask her for my mother's address. Uh, it's important to get my GED scores sent home."

Home—an image quite transient in David's head. Brooklyn, Hempstead, Queens. In between, it could be any number of JDCs (juvenile detention centers). A nomad in an urban desert.

"Sure, David, What's her name? And number?" I copied the information onto a piece of paper. I would try to reach her and find out where they were living now.

David didn't know the outcome of his case yet; but when he got his GED, it was important that he have an address for the certificate to be mailed to. It was important that he find someone in his life who would stay long enough at one mailing address to receive it—just in case he didn't make it back home.

David barely fit in the blue plastic chair across from me. His long legs sprawled in front of him, and he squirmed, rather than sat, as we talked. He leaned so far forward in front of himself that his back U-turned to face me. I could only see his two eyes poking over the front of the desk. From my perspective, David looked like a five-year-old peeking from over the edge.

"Do you want to know a secret, Mrs. Z?"

Secret, I thought. Inmates don't want to share secrets. Secrets are their only plan of escape.

David led the way. "I never went to high school." A simple statement. He smiled. The same smile that he shone when he was trying to convince me that he had lost a book. This one delighted in its own success—to pull a fast one, to double deal, to con. "I never went to high school, Mrs. Z, and I still took the GED." He grinned.

"I mean, I went to school, sort of, in those JDCs. They had us read books and take tests sometimes and stuff, but like I never went to a real school after eighth grade. I really studied hard to pass this test." He took pride in this informal assessment. He straightened up. The adult sat up in his chair.

"Well, it paid off. You worked really hard, David. You should congratulate yourself."

We both grinned at each other. Not quite knowing who was the winner or what hand we were playing. Only knowing that we were both feeling pretty damn good. Congratulations, David.

"Shakespeare was naturally learned; he needed not the spectacles of books to read nature. He looked inwards, and found her there."
—John Dryden

Chapter 6

"All the world's a stage"

And there are the Davids, the Hectors, the Diquans, all mysteries being slowly revealed. Small clues are provided by the boys, not prior test scores or parents' telephone calls. There are many like David who are their own guardians, even at sixteen or seventeen. Besides, the court has already defined them as adults. It doesn't matter that I can see them as just kids. Most people don't want to see that. Most people don't want to admit that they gave up on them long before they ever arrived here. Schools and social workers and psychologists already know. Family structure significantly predicts delinquency. And by sixth grade, schools are able to identify high school dropouts. So long before David started his trips to family court, the system knew that his destiny might be doomed. They were crossing their fingers that he might end up among the 58 percent who make it out. He didn't. He's in the 42 percent who end up in places like this. Over and over and over again.

So David gives me a clue: his family life isn't stable. Stories build as trust does. There are no backstories, no commentators providing analysis. This is not a reality TV show. Over time, I might get something more, maybe not. A lot of what I do is by instinct. Well before David confides in me about his mother, I know that his time spent in the one or two or three JDCs around New York State meant that he hadn't been spending a lot of time at home.

What you see is what you get. I am just grateful for our connection. I can't hope for more. David could be locked in tomorrow, or sent to BMU (Behavior Management Unit), or be sent home. What happens overnight determines who shows up tomorrow. Last night's altercations determine today's attendance. I don't have to follow a running narrative about David's beginning, middle, and end. Most of these boys' beginnings are about the same: fatherless family, poor, sketchy educational background—either learning or discipline problems, or both. More than a quarter of inmates cited behavioral or disciplinary actions as the reason they dropped out of school in the first place. Schools know that 71 percent of all high school dropouts come from fatherless homes—nine times the average; and like David, 39 percent of jail inmates live in mother-only households. Oh, there are variations on the same theme, but there is a composite sketch—a little boy holding tenaciously onto a mother's skirt, who is really struggling to make it in this world. Little boys who are forced to grow up real quick. Little boys who get pushed around a lot. Boys who try and try and try, but never succeed.

So David's getting the GED IS a big deal—even though he doesn't realize it. There are a million studies, but they all agree that one of the reasons David is in here is because he hadn't finished high school. Almost 75 percent of America's state prison inmates, close to 59 percent of federal inmates, and nearly 69 percent of jail inmates did not complete high school. If given the chance to get their GEDs, their chances for recidivism—making the return trip—drops 33 percent. David was proud of his accomplishment, as well he should be, but what he doesn't realize is how much he's increasing his odds of not coming back.

What most people don't realize, what most taxpayers don't, what most of my friends who grumble to me about how somehow being in jail is beating the system—"two hots and a cot"—is how much they save by David's getting his GED. There's a payoff for them, too: according to criminal justice experts, Levin & Kilpatrick, that increase in schooling will reduce murder and assault rates by almost 30 percent, motor vehicle theft by 20 percent, arson by 13 percent, and burglary and larceny by about 6 percent. Quite a value all around. David's wheeling and dealing is as natural to him as my looking for all the answers in a book. Both of us have to adjust our approaches if we're going to survive. David's discovering that some of the answers are on more solid ground—like in a book. And I'm finding that, here at least, some of the answers are found in a more gut-level, knee-jerk response. Jail is changing me, too.

The Davids, the Hectors, the Diquans come and go. I catch glimpses of them as they pass through our school with no notion that I will be present for the finale. What was it that Shakespeare said? "All the world's a stage, and all the men and women merely players: They have their exits and their entrances; and one man in his time plays many parts…"

Of course, I rely on a quote in an attempt to explain it. David's recent note explains it far better instead: "Hey, Mrs. Z, ya gotta get me some books 'cause they put me on lock-in. Keep trying to call my sister."

People come and go. He learned that early on without the benefit of any degree. I'm just learning it now.

"Success is not final, failure is not fatal: it is the courage to continue that counts."
—Winston Churchill

Chapter 7

Francisco

Not everyone wants to get out of jail. Seriously.

I happened to call over to the Yaphank jail today, trying to get hold of the GED teacher over there. Long story short, there's an inmate in the drug treatment program who wants to take his GED exam—but had already taken the GED prep classes there.

Some students come to class as a break from the all-pervasive boredom of jail life, yet there are others who want to finish what they've started. They want to make the changes necessary to reframe their lives. To get out and make a clean start.

Francisco had the look in his black eyes. A sad, tired look that you shouldn't see in someone so young, but eyes that still glimmered with life, with determination, with a willingness to start all over again.

His counselor was calling in a favor to get him to take the exam. Ivan knew that Francisco had bumped his way past our age limit of twenty-one while he was bumping his way around from Yaphank to Hudson, and back to us again. Francisco's using and abusing was using and abusing him. But Francisco was back. Up until he was twenty-one, Francisco had been guaranteed an education through New York State Education Law.

When I met him, my first thought—how gentle he is. Soft spoken. Well mannered. Respectful.

"Yes, ma'am." … "No, ma'am."

You'd never imagine a needle in his arm. Coke on the table in front of him. You'd never imagine him doing anyone any harm.

"Do you remember the last time you took a practice test? What was your score?"

I'd probe a little to see if he even was a candidate for the GED.

He'd done pretty well: all 500s. A sure pass. All he needed was a minimum of 410 on each of the five subtests and a total test score of 2250. He deserved to give it a shot.

"But, I got a problem, miss. I'm waiting for a bed."

"I don't understand, Francisco. Where are you waiting for a bed?"

"Phoenix House."

"That's great, Francisco. I don't see a problem." I'm a strong proponent for the axiom, let the punishment fit the crime. Drug rehab is certainly a more appropriate and better alternative for a drug user than incarceration. I didn't see this as a problem.

"No, miss, you don't understand—what about if they get me a bed before the GED? I want to stay in jail until after the GED exam."

I remembered writing a letter to a judge, asking if a student's sentencing could be put off for two weeks so he could stay to take the GED. That's how important it was to him. The judge let him stay.

That piece of paper was damn important to some of those boys. For some, it meant the ability to enlist in the military, or apply to college, or even get a job. All keys to succeeding on the outside. But most of all, it was the difference between piloting a nosedive or regaining control.

Francisco was trying to regain control. Even if it meant his staying in jail an extra month or two.

You see it in some students. It might be their second or third time around. They may have been upstate and back. Life may have been a cruel teacher. But there is a conviction in their eyes that you know is truth. They're going to make it.

The other boys wander into the classroom and slouch down at their desks. The last thing on their minds—school. Maybe, talking to the guy three cells down. Reading a newspaper. Getting out. Just bullshitting. Getting away with as much as a school jail will allow.

But not the Franciscos—now desperate to succeed. They move differently. They go directly to their desk, pick up their work, and focus on it. And prep and study as they've never done before. This time, they will succeed. This time, they won't come back. This time, they will move forward with their lives.

But chances for rehabilitation are rare. The system is a system bound up in pain, not passage.

Inmates are transferred. Like Francisco. They start, they don't finish. They're transferred again. Their school records are not. And they have to start all over again. Inmates are released. Almost there. Maybe, two days before the test. Left nowhere.

Which is why I'm on the phone today. Francisco had taken a practice test in Yaphank last fall. He was that close to taking the GED—two practice tests passed, registration complete, and the test only a week away when he was transferred upstate to Hudson Correctional Facility.

Then he started all over again. At Hudson. In a new GED class. And now—he's afraid he's going to find a bed—a much-needed bed, but, again, a couple of days short of the exam.

I called Yaphank. His teacher there remembered him. Tells you something about Francisco.

She was rallying 'round him. "God bless any one of them when they go out of their way to try and finish their educations. You know," she reminded me, "education is key."

I didn't need to be reminded. Neither did she.

"I'll look through the files and try to get his scores to you as soon as I can."

Francisco took the exam. And even though there's hardly a happy ending here, he passed—with a score well above average, I might add.

The CO brought him to the school office to get his GED certificate, and I saw him.

"Hey, Mrs. Z, ya hear I passed."

"Congratulations, Francisco." I could see and sense something different in him. His eyes didn't look so tired. He didn't seem so bent. For once, life hadn't beaten him down. For now.

Francisco and I both knew it would be different on the outside. Life was still waiting for him out there. Even with his GED in hand.

But when you do one good thing for yourself, then you can do another and another and another, and ... who knows what Francisco had waiting for him out there with his GED in hand? Next time, life might be different. Next time.

"The very existence of libraries affords the best evidence
that we may yet have hope for the future of man."
—T. S. Eliot

Chapter 8

Philanthropy

From a librarian's viewpoint, our students are a select group, requiring a select collection of books. I, for one, would not necessarily promote the newer, more-select genres, such as urban fiction, exclusively. Giving them things to read that they will read is what will keep them reading.

That's how the whole book cart started in the first place. Who would have thought that a conversation over a cup of coffee with a friend would have led to this cart full of books—all kinds of books. One cup of coffee with my friend Margaret, and making the connection with her son, Will Dennis at DC Comics, led to their donations and the foundations of our now-burgeoning library. Most libraries are built by budgets or philanthropic endowments, but ours has been growing in leaps and bounds by word-of-mouth endorsements. A cup of coffee. A son in the book industry. A friend working in a library. A brother-in-law with a lot of book donations.

But beggars can't be choosers. My librarian friend, Donna, in the high school (thank God, I've found loads of them) mentioned she had a rolling book cart she wasn't using. Was I interested?

I had been wondering what to do with all those comic book donations and, like a prayer answered, Donna and her book cart appeared.

The next day, there were the two of us rolling it outside the school and trying to shove it sideways into the back of my SUV. Two of the wheels kept falling out of what I think you call caster clips. But this was a clandestine operation. The book cart was on loan, having been requisitioned for the high school library, not intended for me. We moved as stealthily as the CIA.

Book cart in tow and now Donna-less, I pulled into the back lot of the jail. Getting it out solo was even a greater accomplishment. Before I knew it—it was rolling. And has been rolling ever since.

That slightly crooked oak, three-shelf-high cart heralded our new library. It creaked and clunked down the hall, carrying whatever we could put on its back. Like a day laborer willing to endure whatever work would pay. And like those who labor every day, bending their backs, brushing sweat from their brow, doing whatever it takes to do whatever job, like those who break, who wear out, who wither before they should, our book cart did, too. Its wheel cracked off. A shelf caved in. It didn't roll.

But it had birthed a library. As much as the farm worker plants a seed, it, too, had planted something good, something life-giving, something nourishing.

Our program director soon after requisitioned a book cart all our own. Four shelves high, two sided, four sturdy wheels, chrome. Just to my specifications. One side, fiction and English. The other, nonfiction and Spanish. The separation of fact and fate.

Our library had been born. A ragtag collection of thumbed-over pages and folded-over bookmarks. Coffee-stained periodicals. *People* magazines with yesterday's wives. Comics. And as we move forward, brand new books we're ordering. A wonderful and growing rich collection of perennials and colorful annuals of books.

There's a lot of weeding out, of course. People's generosity doesn't necessarily reflect our students' reading interests. *The Devil Wears Prada* might have made it to the *Times* bestseller list, but it is not going to grab anyone's interest here. If it did, I'd be shaking those pages out, for sure, to see if there was something else besides a bookmark inside!

Truth is, I'll take books from anywhere and get recommendations from almost anyone, too. Check them out afterward. Unlike most librarians, I don't have the time to peruse the *School Library Journal*—for that matter, even the *Times Book Review*.

Sometimes, recommendations are a surprise. Where I get them. And from whom.

It's after school, and I'm rushing through Union Square to meet my daughter for dinner. I eye a street vendor selling used DVDs, and since I had been looking for a copy of *The Manchurian Candidate* that afternoon online anyway, and since I have a few minutes to spare, I decide to stop and ask.

I explain I want to use it in my high school class for a lesson on Election Day.

The guy tells me he has two copies and starts to

look through his assortment of 100 boxes. As he shuffles through his disorganized, unalphabetized collection, he looks up. "You want a movie to show your high school kids?" He shoves a copy of the DVD, *The Legend of Bobby Z,* in my hand. I've never heard of it.

I start reading the back summary. Interesting content. Ironically, it's about a convict. A DEA agent. Right up my students' alley. But looks too violent for my taste. "I'm sure my students would love it, but I'd get fired for showing it." I laugh.

"Why?"

"Well, I work in a high school program in a jail."

"Which one?" He looks at me now like he's an expert on the various locations of the NYS Department of Corrections.

I tell him.

"Oh, I've been there." He confesses or, should I say provides, without hesitation. "I know what you mean. Suppression." In a liberation kind of way, he continues, "They should be able to see things they like to see."

I don't necessarily disagree.

I exchange the money for *The Manchurian Candidate.* But turn to the ex-con/DVD vendor, "Well, I do at least try and get them books they like to read."

"Well, then, get them anything by Don Wilson," he suggests. "Have you tried Paul Langan's *Bluford High* series? My nephew loves them."

"Hold on." I fumble in my bag for a pen and paper so I can write this all down.

He is dumbfounded. He doesn't expect me to take him seriously. He's used to his words spinning into the cyclone of words and jive and rap and come-ons circling Union Square.

With my paper and pen in hand, I start to write down the authors' names and his recommendations.

Who knows what kind of authors he's just given me, or what kind of books. I'll check them out tomorrow. For now, they represent potential bestsellers for "the cart." They mightn't be Pulitzer Prize winners, but they will probably be closer to what the students want to read than anything I know about.

I close my pad and put it back in my bag and smile.

"Thank you, ma'am," is all he says. There's a look of pride on his face. As if he's just done something useful and productive for society. He knows that there's something good about what he's just done. And there is.

He walks back to his DVD table, vending his wares. I walk down University Place with a pocket full of book recommendations. Both of us are satisfied customers.

The next day, when I go to play *The Manchurian Candidate*, the disc is blank. Somehow, I don't feel so swindled.

"I'm not an angel, Jace," she repeated. "I don't return library books. I steal illegal music off the Internet. I lie to my mom. I am completely ordinary."
—Cassandra Clare, *City of Glass*

Chapter 9

Dyshone

I hate to admit this, but I once accrued a $125 library fine. After a foot operation, I limped to the Brooklyn Public Library with my overdue book in hand and pleaded my case ..." I wasn't able to drive. I couldn't walk. I had no one to return it for me."

Some of it was true. Mostly, I had forgotten to bring the book back, but the library cut a deal. I took it. I pleaded out.

They reduced the fine. I paid. Life went on.

Life in court, of course, isn't all that simple. Nothing in real life is that simple.

Hurricane Sandy had really socked the living daylights out of Long Island. The jail sat right in the center of all of the devastation—the flooding to its south, the wind storm to the north, and the electric outages all around. For once, there was an advantage to being here. Backup generators insured our inmates electricity and heat that our neighbors didn't have for weeks.

So I did notice the Long Beach address when I got Dyshone's intake form—Long Beach had really been hit.

I immediately wondered if he was arrested before or after the storm. In fact, it was one of the first things I asked.

"How'd you and your family make out during the storm? Is everyone safe?"

"Well, I'm not positive, but I think they've been able to move back to our house this week." An old man's sense of worry furrowed across his brow but quickly smoothed itself out. "They really don't have a phone, but I spoke to my grandmother two nights ago, and they've been moving some stuff back."

This old man's apparition often surfaced upon many of the boys' faces and then disappeared. Their faces wore the old man's worry or his pain like a thespian's masque until they could find the strength to find a disguise of their own. Dyshone took a moment or two to compose himself. "I'm sure they're fine. Nobody's bothered to call me." And he stepped back into character.

I had to imagine him, though, as I often tried to imagine these boys when they stepped outside these walls. When I tried to imagine what they looked like when not dressed in their creamsicle orange.

Dyshone was tall and solid, probably difficult to blow over in a storm. His dark ebony skin looked as polished as some of the beach glass I used to find near the shore at Long Beach. The way he let his uniform hang was probably the way his pants hung, too—low, probably too low for his mother's taste. He walked slow—like the thin bubbly foam that seeps beneath the sand after a crashing wave has rushed hurriedly away. It was easy to imagine Dyshone if he was out of here. I'd imagine he wasn't that bad a kid. Not perfect. But not too bad.

It had already been about a month since Sandy had passed, and so many families still hadn't been able to move back to their homes and were as sprinkled as the tree limbs that the storm had left behind. Sandy cost an estimated $71 billion in damages. The TV cameras scanning the bent wooden beams of wall-less beach houses said one thing. Boys like Dyshone said another.

"Were you home or here when the storm hit, Dyshone?" I asked, not certain that being here was necessarily the safer of the two.

"Home—I wasn't picked up until last week."

We had just returned from Thanksgiving break. For many families on Long Island, like Dyshone's, a Thanksgiving filled with blessed confusion ... the gratitude of receiving only minor damages instead of major destruction. I was sure that Dyshone's arrest compounded those damages.

"Where is your family living now?"

"All over. My little brother went down South—to Virginia to stay with my aunt. My mother and sister are in Long Beach. And my grandmother, she is staying with someone from church."

And Dyshone was staying here. I had already checked his charges—E felony, trespassing and criminal intent. Resisting arrest. Probation violation. Sentenced to sixty days.

"What kind of lawyer do you have?" I knew already that it couldn't have been "paid." A paid lawyer would have meant that it had the added benefit of affording his $750 bail. Dyshone could afford neither.

"When were you arrested before?" I wondered how long he had lasted on probation. Statistics already had predicted his violation. By 2008, when New York City stopped slapping on long probation periods for everything from misdemeanors to A felonies, their probation population declined 43 percent. Outside of New York City, where Dyshone now was doing his time, the numbers remained the same. For Dyshone, it was always the same—wrong place, wrong time.

I added, "How long have you been on probation?"

"A year, ma'am. I was arrested last year for trespassing and criminal intent. My brother and me got caught in an abandoned house down by the bay. It had a For Sale sign and stuff, but we weren't supposed to be in there."

"And did you get a YO—a youthful offender?"

A nod.

"Good," I said. That YO was his gift from the court, his ticket out of Dodge, his freedom pass. That YO meant his records would be sealed unless ... he broke probation, which this arrest did.

I jotted onto my notepad: Prior YO. Legal Aid lawyer. E felony. ???

"Did your lawyer explain the possibility of dropping your charge from a felony to a misdemeanor?"

Alphabet soup. A felony. B. C felony. D. E felony. Misdemeanor.

Oh, I'm sure cops, COs, and newspaper reporters understand. It is something that has to be learned. I'm learning, too.

Like a primer. And the boys learn how to run the felony stairs.

Their recitations, pretty much the same:

"They're dropping it from a C to a D, Mrs. Z," he said with such a relieved sigh ...

Or the solutions jumbled, "if they lower the B to a C, then I only have to do county time—cutting some months off of the sentence.

Like slurping alphabet soup. Pleading from A to B or C to D, or a felony to a misdemeanor. Avoiding chance and trial. Like my library fine.

They'll cut a deal. They'll plead out. Maybe only have to do some time.

And an E is as easy as sixty days. And county time is only two-thirds the days. So for Dyshone, only between Thanksgiving and Christmas—well, a little bit more.

And for the DA, fewer trials. For the courts, one less case on the docket. And for the defendant, not having to spend a lot of money on a lawyer. But Dyshone doesn't have a lot of money to spend on a lawyer anyway. He hasn't saved anything.

"Didn't your lawyer suggest …?"

Before I could finish, Dyshone answered. "Yeah, he did. But there was a mistake." (Always a mistake). "It was supposed to be a misdemeanor—but when I got to court they said it was still a felony."

"Who?" I asked. Who had made the mistake?

A mistake, defined, is something easily removed—perhaps, with the other end of your pencil. Erasing a D and replacing it with an E. Or changing a felony to a misdemeanor.

But Dyshone's sentence wasn't a mistake. That E felony couldn't be erased.

Something his lawyer forgot to tell him before Dyshone so quickly jumped.

Much like a permanent tattoo, that felony, no matter what the letter, wouldn't fade.

Whether Dyshone was seventeen or nineteen or twenty-two.

"My lawyer said I should wait and appeal the plea and come back to court another day. He didn't know how long that would be."

And youth, lacking patience, got in the way. Youth stood right in front of wisdom's path. Of course.

"I just wanna get outta here ... I can't wait that long."

Dyshone just wanted to get it all out of the way ... off his plate. In a world of jailhouse lawyers, self-appointed members of the bar, felonies are graded much like octane levels. Dyshone did not see his E felony or sixty days as harmful. Slow him up a bit, but not clog his engine. Much better than a D and a year.

"But what I'm really pissed about is that I'm going to miss my birthday and Christmas. The judge set my release date for December 28th."

I looked up into this seventeen-year-old's face. One day before Halloween, a storm blew in and swept away his home. A town was lost in its surge. A community already broken to begin with and, divided by rich and poor, was now broken more. And he was being swept out to sea.

The day Dyshone walked into court, I don't know if anyone noticed the date or time or address attached to his name. Yes, he did break the imposed curfew caused by Sandy. He was out after 7:00 p.m. Yes, he was on probation and they took him in. Maybe someone could have thrown him a rescue line—maybe, cut him a deal instead of anchoring him to a felony for the rest of his days.

They had to know that a felony, even an E, would weigh him down: difficulties with college financial aid, licenses, bonding, no hope of dreaming limitless dreams.

For Dyshone, these felony stairs stood still. This arrest, if he managed to be good, was sealed—he'd yet to celebrate his eighteenth birthday. For others, not so lucky. Birthdays are unkind here. Youth's foolishness has strict boundaries and definitions.

I need to think, I really do, that Dyshone could have been more than a docket number that day. Maybe something besides a gavel, a felony, and a slamming cell door might have done him more good.

Someone might have seen Dyshone limping in as much as I. And cut him a deal. Let him pay his sixty days somewhere else, or in some other way. And let his life go on.

"In the depth of winter I finally learned that there was in me an invincible summer."
—Albert Camus

Chapter 10

Hurricanes and Other Disasters

Disasters like Hurricane Sandy, though, come in all shapes and sizes. For Dyshone, it was one of the biggest hurricanes to hit the Northeast that brought him and his family down. They weren't alone—Sandy forced 776,000 people in the Northeast out of their homes. Turns out, it was the world's third largest displacement in 2012, following a massive flood in India and a typhoon in China. But Dyshone and his family had been displaced many times before. This time, they really had no place to go.

Rallying for my belief in outreach services, the few places Dyshone's family could have gone after the storm on Long Island were some of Nassau County's libraries. They served as warming stations, Internet connections to the outside world, and in some cases, like Freeport, one of the few places around with enough electricity to charge your cellphone. In Long Beach, though, they weren't so lucky.

But disasters don't have to be weather-related or have anything to do with nature. We expect damages from hurricanes and earthquakes. We don't see the damages from the other disasters in our lives—normal everyday occurrences that can ravage the human spirit as much as torrential rain or wind gusts.

Dyshone is displaced and disconnected from his grandmother, from his mother, and from the rest of his family. He doesn't know where his father is. The hurricane just tore up all of the threads that were already unraveling.

When my first husband died, it was like that, too. Illness and death and grief can combine into a powerful and forceful storm surge. They churn the seas and pound upon life's deck. My three children and I were cast to sea.

I never imagined the havoc that would enter our lives or what I would have to do to restore some sanity in our lives. But I did. My sons thought they had become men. Just like most of the boys here, they were really very hurt and confused young men. There were the same calls from school about attendance, the failing grades, the climbing in and out of windows beyond disregarded curfews. They still needed direction when they perceived they needed none. My family was drowning at sea, and I was desperately seeking some kind of rescue. I thought that I might find help in the juvenile courts. Instead, I found the courts drowning in their own angry sea—overcrowded dockets, overwrought court-appointed guardians, and helpless mothers just like me. There wasn't a lot of help out there. I suspect that hasn't changed a lot.

I think of that tumultuous time in my life when I meet each boy. I don't forget it. It reminds me that my life is not so different from any one of theirs. *There, but for the grace of God go I . . .*

I think about Diquan. He's been coming to school since his brother's funeral, but he hasn't been the same. He doesn't joke as often when I poke my head in; he hasn't been asking for so many books. I don't know what he's been doing with his time. I hope he's been writing—but he hasn't asked for another notebook. Life's disasters take many forms.

I think about where my sons are today, too. I think of them as successful businessmen, as good husbands, as the wonderful people they are; and I remember that the boys I meet can be all of those things, too. They aren't so different from my own sons.

Those boys aren't so different from me. Or from my daughter. Or from anyone who has ever lived through the human catastrophe called life.

What makes Dyshone or most of the other boys different from my sons is what they don't have to survive.

Dyshone's family doesn't have a house right now, but they don't have a lot of other things, either. They don't have the benefits of education that my family had. He probably doesn't have the benefit of role models—someone to just put an arm around his shoulder and nudge him in the right direction.

My boys had plenty of people nudging them along. They needed time to act out their emotional pain. Truth is, I needed time to process my own.

These boys need time, too. Most of them just need to talk and talk and talk. I am willing to listen, but one person times 150 boys who are constantly being arrested or released—one boy out, one new one in—doesn't give me a lot of time for listening. I know I need to sit down and talk to Diquan—I want to know how he's doing and, more important, if he's going home. His mother could use having her one son back. I need to contact Dyshone's high school—find out if we can keep up with his schoolwork, but they've moved. The whole building was under water a month ago.

My rolling cart gives me the time I need to spend with the boys. At each classroom door I roll into, there are six hellos, six quick scans of the room, six opportunities for them to ask to speak to me, or six opportunities for me to talk to them. There are usually three or four requests for books, too. The common denominator among us all.

So hurricanes come and go. Things are swept out to sea. People lose each other. There is pain. It is the human condition, and my students suffer it earlier than they should. My children suffered it earlier than they should have, too. That happens sometimes.

People react in as many ways as there are people on this earth. Sometimes, they become presidents in spite of the pain; and sometimes, they get in trouble because of the pain. Life can be painful no matter how it motivates you. With the kids here, life has had a way of steering them in the wrong direction; they haven't learned the navigational skills to steer any other way.

I grieve for all of them—my own children and these children of others.

Dyshone will spend his sixty days. He will spend his lifetime remembering it. Right now, I am hoping he can go on with it without carrying that felony.

For all of them, I hope they can move on with their lives without being weighed down by the grief and mistakes that came before.

I understand. I am not that different from them.

"Life's under no obligation to give us what we expect."
—Margaret Mitchell

Chapter 11

Kourtney and the Boys in Classroom 4

Every library's budget builds in an accepted amount of loss. Loss due to damage. Loss due to unforeseen circumstances—water pipes breaking or a coffee cup spilt across a shelf—and of course, for all of us sinners, unreturned books. Those books gathering dust somewhere under a bed, or the others left in the back of a bus, or the others floating out to sea as the tide comes in. It is no different here, but for reasons far more creative.

This afternoon, the boys in classroom 4 asked that the cart be brought down. I'd been out two days and not attending to it well, and its collection was rather scant. But I wheeled it down anyway and knew there'd be complaints.

"I was looking for comics. There's no new ones." A disappointed face.

"What happened to *Twilight*? Who has that book out?" I grab my index card box—my twenty-first century cataloging system utilizing Melvil Dewey-esque technological aids: pen, paper, and a decimal system, and started on a mission to get book backs, starting with room 4.

Kourtney's card comes up first—"Kourtney, you owe *Twilight*."

He answers, "It's not my fault—it's the county's."

"The county's?" Are they passing *Twilight* around the County Executive Office?"

"No, but when I was released Friday, they took all my things. And when they rearrested me Saturday, it was all gone with all the rest of my stuff. Some CO is reading *Twilight* now."

One definite loss. Kourtney was right. We were not getting that book back anytime soon. Ridiculously, I knew he probably could walk out the door Friday feeling freed to be picked up on Saturday on an old charge and a newly issued warrant. The system created a revolving door for him.

Our most popular books walk. And I'm not certain I'm really upset about it. (My God, this would make me an outcast in the library world). *The 100 Most Amazing Places on the Planet, How They Croaked (How the 100 Most Famous People Died)* and *The Shack*, a murder mystery masking a spiritual and inspirational tone and message of forgiveness, are real hits.

The boys beg for those books; and unfortunately, when they walk, it's tough to replace them.

One morning, we arrive to our office only to find two huge black plastic bags filled with books, some ours, some not. There had been a shakedown, when cells are emptied of all belongings and some things thrown back. Mattresses are overturned; letters and photographs are thrown onto a heap in the middle of the floor and tossed. Possessions become common property, and property no longer is yours.

Obviously, there are good security reasons for the shakedowns—books are ideal hiding places and a great conveyance for "kites," messages between inmates. There's a rumor of a concealed weapon, or someone's managed to smuggle in drugs. If only our books weren't lost in the process.

If my grandmother had mentioned the adage that an idle mind is the devil's workshop, she couldn't have imagined what creative activities manifest themselves within an idle mind locked in most of the day. Probably, one of the biggest threats in a jail population is the idle mind. I am only an educator working within a jail and only an observer; but in just a short time, I realized the power and threat of that idleness.

Then there are the weeks when those books just walk and never come back.

Those are the weeks when books are always in the greatest demand—the weeks before vacation, during holidays, when the time between court dates and when you get out becomes 300 pages longer and three books more than you thought.

I forget about those weeks. Or I forget about the boys, and the books, and the jail some weeks.

This past week, I counted the days until our two-week vacation. It'd been a long summer, one wrought with my own family difficulties and problems. I needed a break.

Michael's back in the hospital. Again. He's gotten yet one more infection. They were having a difficult enough time combating the staph infection; now, he's picked up something called Klebisella—very dangerous and very antibiotic resistant.

And the worst news possible—my sister Irene died. There are no words to express this loss. With an extended illness like hers, it is one of those things you expect, but then don't. Hope always has you clinging onto the belief that she has one more day.

I can't believe my youngest sister is dead. There's something unnatural about it. I'm the oldest. All of our lives, we've done things in age order—graduation, marriage, children. Her death was not supposed to precede mine. I keep looking at the picture of the five of us seated in an age order, size order line, and can't imagine her *Photoshopped* from the picture.

To make matters worse, on the exact same day, I got a call from the rehabilitation center that they were taking Michael by ambulance back to the hospital again. Just when I thought he was finally improving, that he might be making his way out toward some kind of recovery, he was moving backward again. I don't know how many more months of IVs or therapy this will start all over again. All I know is that it's been a long year.

I'm exhausted. The last thing I am really thinking about today is the boys or the books. I need a break. Actually, I need a vacation. All I have to look forward to over the next few days is a wake, a funeral, and what has now become a ritual—trips back and forth to the hospital.

The book cart collection was a little sparse, and I was a little slack in my collection notices. *Oh, I'll get around to it when we get back. When was Friday again?*

But each time I'd pass a classroom, there'd be one boy or another begging for the cart to be brought in. They'd insist, "We won't be in school next week."

I wanted to shout, "I know we won't!" What seemed a glorious idea to me was not seeming glorious to them. How differently perspective colors how we see the world. It dawned on me that these students, so many of them truants or dropouts, now were concerned about our two-week break.

When I passed classroom 4, there was only one boy who had come up that morning with the minors, and he had asked to see me. I wheeled the cart into the room and sat across from him. "Were you looking for anything specific to read, Martin?"

"No, miss. I wanted to talk to you. That's all." Martin wasn't one of my usual talkers. He would be described as taciturn by the appreciative observer, and hostile by most. Today, he seemed preoccupied.

Martin went on to explain that he was used to talking to his grandmother a lot of the time, and he hadn't seen her for a long time. He was feeling very sad. He wasn't sleeping and was getting up in the middle of the night and throwing up. He talked and he talked. And I listened. He explained how he was trying to think of ways to kill himself. In school, he thought about stealing one of the teachers' pens from a desk when they weren't looking. That is one of the reasons none of us really carry regular pens or regular pencils, for that matter. Regardless of method, Martin was having suicidal thoughts. This was an immediate mental health referral.

I could recommend books. I could tell him what exams to study. I could call his grandmother and ask for her to visit. But what could I say to a seventeen-year-old who I knew was facing some very serious charges and a long stay in prison? I listened. I kept thinking about Irene and Michael, and before that, my husband John, and how disordered life was. And I was looking at Martin and wondering why someone would want to end his life at seventeen. I kept listening.

Martin talked. I listened. And then I told him how concerned I was. That he needed to talk to a professional and that I not only would like to help him connect but that I was obligated to help him connect. I told him it didn't make a difference—whether I had to or if I didn't—I wanted him to get help. He didn't have to be living with that much pain. He nodded his head in agreement. I told him I'd take care of it, and it would be okay.

Martin knew I didn't have any simple solution to slap onto his life. He didn't expect me to come up with one. When he had finished talking, though, he did want a book from the cart.

I wished I had one that would offer him all the things he was looking for and all of the things he needed—comfort, counsel, and most of all, a future. Instead, he chose *Al Capone Does My Shirts*, a whimsical account of a young boy growing up on Alcatraz, marketing laundry services using Al Capone's name, and a James Patterson novel—perhaps not the most demanding reads, but certainly, worry free. Martin seemed pleased with the selections and relieved to have talked to me.

I spoke with the CO, and they called over to Mental Health. Martin would be taken care of—for now.

I got up to leave, and I didn't care so much about all of those missing books. I didn't care about my own problems. They didn't seem such big problems. I was just glad that

Martin had felt enough of a connection between me and those books to open those pages on that part of his life today.

"The past does not have to be your prison. You have a voice in your destiny. You have a say in your life. You have a choice in the path you take."
—Max Lucado, *When God Whispers Your Name*

Chapter 12

Dawuan

You can't judge a book by its cover. Or a kid by the way he looks.

When Dawuan first came to us on loan from Rikers Island, he was a lot more than intimidating. Not to mention that he was a giant. Dawuan was built like some of the finest linebackers I have ever seen—wide all around, tall, and impossible to get by. And if his God-given physique wasn't going to stop you, his attitude would.

His jaw was squared to his neck as a tightly as a screw to a nut. His head barely moved from side to side. He just stared intently and intensely.

He was solid as stone. Silent. Mrs. P could barely catch his name when he first came into the class, and it didn't look like he cared to give it out much to anyone. He was minding his business, and we should mind ours.

But the books we read do tell a lot about us. And the ones Dawuan read did as well.

The book cart rolled into the room, and Dawuan barely raised his head. Everyone else dodged for the cart.

71

Dawuan, however, was working quietly in a self-imposed solitary in front of one of the computer screens.

Before I exited, I approached him. "Do you want to sign something out before vacation?" We (the teachers) were about to have a week off; the students, however, were not.

He hesitated—for a second—just enough for me to find that empty pocket to run through.

He got up and looked through the books left on the cart—not much after the other boys had chosen their beach reads. Dawuan held up one of the donated books—*Framed*. On its cover, a forlorn-looking Doberman pinscher in jail stripes was poking his head between the bars of his cell.

"Do you think it's funny?" he asked. He signed it out.

This week Dawuan asked me if I could call his mom— he'd been having trouble getting through, and he said it was urgent. I don't have, nor have to have, the particulars, but Dawuan's experience behind bars has not been that fun. Regardless of his attitude or size.

He was moved all around Rikers before moving to the suburbs, if that's how you want to describe our county jail. He was in a gang and went out against the gang when they did something against his family. That was enough, I think, to get him to cooperate with the authorities and offer his family some security, but it hasn't offered him the same inside.

Gang activity is as much a threat here as it is on the streets. And our classrooms acknowledge that fact. Last month, some expert outside educator, came in for a visit and suggested cooperative learning activities. What she saw was a group of students, similarly aged, from diverse educational experiences and intellectual levels. The next logical question would then become: how can we pair each student to best optimize the shared learning experience? How can we provide differentiated instruction, providing similar material at different learning stages and levels? Here, the most obvious question becomes: Can we pair each student to optimize any experience? Sometimes, a pairing or a group is not cooperative at all. It looks an awful lot like a rumble.

So, today, Dawuan called his mother and told her to contact the ADA, assistant district attorney. There are rumblings going on between gangs here. Someone from The City recognized him and asked who he was. Dawuan's feeling uncomfortable. He doesn't want to be hurt, but what he says that is more important is that he wants to get out. He's been moving all over jails and correctional facilities and courts over the last two years. He's close to serving time. The last thing he needs is to catch a charge—that is, get another charge added to the one he has. An assault on another prisoner. Or one on a CO. Or I am sure other charges I can't even think of. He can. He knows how a gang can strike back. In ways that are far subtler than violent, by letting him catch another charge and keeping him locked in, locked in a very unsafe place. In a sense "framed." Like the book he borrowed.

After the call, Dawuan asked me if he could still go to school if he asked for PC, protective custody. Unfortunately, no. "But there are teachers that do visit for cell study"— although it's very limited.

And I added, "You can still take the GED."

When I spoke with his mother, she so wanted him to get that piece of paper before he came back into the world. Right now, it's not only jail that's keeping him away from it.

"They'll escort you to the exam, Dawuan," I assured him.

I thought about that book he borrowed, and how Dawuan couldn't let anyone know he was looking to laugh. For the last two years, he was living another life—maybe one that he had read about in a book. But not the one that he left behind.

As he walked down the hall, I thought about how different he was from the imposing figure he pretended he was. I thought about how different all of these boys were from the characters they assumed.

No, you can't tell a book by its cover.

"Presence is more than just being there."
—Malcolm Forbes

Chapter 13

"I swear to tell the truth ... the whole truth"

Dawuan never took the GED exam. He was transferred before the exam was ever given. The boys' lives are disrupted like that. Their hopes and dreams, their greatest intentions for turning their lives around, get overturned by somebody else's plans. Besides, it would have taken a lot of red tape to have gotten him to the exam when he was on PC. Not impossible, but difficult.

I try not to disappoint these boys. I try to deliver, I try to show up, to tell the truth. But sometimes, the truth can be awfully discouraging. I try not to be discouraging.

So when Dawuan asks if he can take the GED when he's on PC, I'll assure him that's it's not a problem, even when I know it could be. It's more important that he be safe.

When they ask me for specific books, I don't tell them no, or no way. My librarian friend Donna gave me a long alphabetized Rolodex. I have them write their names along with their requests, and I put it on file. Sometimes, being

77

able to ask for what you want is just as important as getting what you want.

Hector's returned a whole bunch of books from Ad Seg via one of the COs. I don't know if I will be able to funnel him back any more books to read, but I sent him a message that I'd be working on it. I don't know what it's like to be locked up by yourself for months on end, but I'd think that knowing someone was working for you might help you make it to day's end.

It's like that for a lot of things. I tell a severely retarded student who has a tendency to explode and end up in BMU that he probably won't have to wait as long as his computer-assigned court date says. I email a legal aid lawyer to "please make contact at your earliest convenience" and assure the client that it will probably be just a few days though he hasn't had any contact in at least two months.

There's an odd relationship that forms, though, when you do show up—there have been a lot of no-shows in these kids' lives. I think in professional terms, you'd call it accountability, but it was one of the things that surprised me when I first started the library cart.

Before we had our little lending library, the boys certainly read some books. The school had a limited selection, and they simply took the books and rarely returned them. The books went back to the tiers and were never returned.

When I added card jackets, and catalog cards, and had them begin to sign them out, some of the teachers thought I was crazy. "What's the point? They're not going to bring them back."

Well, interestingly, they did. Interestingly, some of

them seemed like they wanted to bring them back. When they were being asked to be accountable, when they were being asked to be responsible and to show up, they wanted to. And when I acknowledged that civic responsibility, they seemed proud, and they wanted to bring those books back even more. It was how our lending library grew. Our books were circulating; they were no longer diminishing.

I was showing up with the cart and I was showing up with some new books. I was listening to their requests and we were building a library and building trust. I never expected this library to be doing so many things. I thought it was going to be about just lending some books.

Sometime afterward, when I surveyed many of them, they hadn't ever owned a library card. They hadn't ever been asked to be accountable before. Turns out, some of them had never visited the public library.

When I used to teach ESL at the high school, I arranged a class trip to the public library. These were kids from foreign countries who weren't used to the concept of a free library system and were being introduced to the public library for the first time. I was amazed at their delight. They went from space to space as if they were visiting Disneyland: free Internet, periodicals, free DVD rentals. They were one of the reasons I went to library school.

I never imagined that there might be American kids who needed to visit the public library. And here they were.

I'd like to take them on a class trip, too. Right now, the cart is as close an experience as they'll have. I don't want to tell them that it isn't even close to the real thing. And that's the truth.

"When you know better, you do better."
—Maya Angelou

Chapter 14

The Shawshank Redemption

Many of the COs don't share my optimism—for the students' success, or for the value of their signing out books.

To be fair, many of them have spent fifteen or twenty years witnessing the same faces going in and out the door. Recidivism is ridiculously high in jails and prisons. The Institute for Higher Education Policy (IHEP) reported that nearly seven in ten people who are formerly incarcerated will commit a new crime, and half will end up back in prison within three years. There are plenty of books on the subject. Very few solutions. Alternatives cost money, and alternatives require a willingness to change. The Rand Institute issued a report in 2013 saying that inmates who had participated in a correctional educational program, like ours, had 43 percent lower odds of recidivating. But correctional educational programs cost money. Books cost money. If my little book cart can prove only one thing, it's that change can happen. We don't have to lock 'em up and throw away the key. But human beings hate change in general and abhor spending their own money on other people's problems—least of all, criminals' problems.

The COs see the books used for a lot of different purposes—besides reading. The most dangerous—a depository for kites, a kind of messenger service within the jail and a huge security breach. What might seem like a harmless form of communication to you and me represents a huge threat to a CO working within. Stress is a silent killer among correction officers and detention officers—what has potential for violence is real and raw, and books can be one of them.

A coordinated jump or attack and a CO's attempt to break it up poses a danger to the intended victim and the CO. There was an average of forty-two assaults by prisoners on jail staff per jail system per month including an average of 206 assaults in each of the seventeen largest jails. That represents an average of four assaults a week. The COs have every reason to be hypervigilant.

So, my optimism and Pollyanna enthusiasm isn't always shared by my non-school coworkers.

"What's the point of giving them books?" one CO asked.

I didn't argue. I knew that for some inmates he was right. For some of them, they'd try and get the heaviest books they could take out. They make the most ideal weights, the closest they can get to makeshift barbells. Lifting weights. Staying in shape is a means of survival here not only an issue of staying healthy.

A lot of COs don't even see the sense of sending these kids to school. The attitude prevails that an education is wasted on someone that is going to spend most of their life in jail. The notion that education might touch a mind, enlarge it, change it, give it a chance to reach behind itself—rehabilitate—elludes them.

They work and have been working in a prison system that has failed to deliver on that notion. You might find the idea written in books or in mission statements, but it remains there on paper.

While it remains on the lines on paper, closed in manuals and textbooks, or discussed in criminal justice classes, COs can't believe that a book might be a means of helping them manage an inmate or reducing the dangers they face on the job. What they mightn't know is that statistics prove that inmates enrolled in school commit 75 percent fewer infractions than inmates not enrolled. That warden after warden has embraced their jail's school programs because they see numerous positive effects: providing an incentive for good behavior; producing mature, well spoken leaders who have a calming influence on others … and sending the message that the institution has some respect for the human potential of incarcerated people.

Until those ideas become realities, the COs I work with will continue to laugh when I roll the cart down the hall.

"Here comes the library lady," one says to the other at the security desk sitting in the middle of our school hallway.

The other snickers, "A regular *Shawshank Redemption*."

They laugh. I roll.

"The eye through which I see God is the same eye through which God sees me; my eye and God's eye are one eye, one seeing, one knowing, one love."
—Meister Eckhart, *Sermons of Meister Eckhart*

Chapter 15

Rodolfo

When I was attending graduate school, a huge discussion ensued on one of our blogs around the time the movie, *The Day After Tomorrow*, was released—another one of those "What do we do at the end of the world?" movies. In our last moments on earth, what becomes most important to us?

In the film, the only safe sanctuary on earth turns out to be the New York Public Library. Heaven for public librarians. The only way to survive, burn books: hell. And the only book to rescue: the Bible.

A lot of people—not just librarians—would argue that the Bible would be the way to save civilization. A lot of people would argue that at least it would be a way to save the soul.

Most people think that there are a lot of souls in here to save, and the Bible would be the book we'd need to save them. They're probably right.

The Bible becomes many things for many people. Comfort. Solace. Forgiveness. Companionship. Someone, not something, to travel with. Everything for some, and nothing for others.

For Rodolfo, it held no interest. Even the promise of chapel didn't get him out of his cell to attend Saturday night services.

As he explained it, "My mother and grandmother do that church stuff. But me and my brother, we don't go. But I know about that Jesus and Maria and some of the *santos*."

He was exempted from Sundays filled with stuffy churches and hatted ladies seated under electric fans.

Not Rodolfo. His family spent whatever time they found together. Not going to church. His family worked hard and long. Not going to church. They sweated all day out in the sun or knelt, scrubbing hardwood floors.

Rodolfo had little time to read the Bible. His faith came from family and food and *futbol*. It was forged in their togetherness and their struggles. It was tested on the streets and the struggle to survive. He knew nothing about the Bible.

So, I thought it odd when he started talking to me about it.

"You know, Mrs. Z. Jesus doesn't want us to have evil thoughts. The devil, he tries to tempt us. The devil always tries to tempt me, but I am going to be better. I am going to be good, I'm not going to listen to him. I've been reading the Bible. I read it every day." He rambled. His eyes looked glazed. His eyes looked empty. Almost vacant.

I smiled.

"I am going to be better, Mrs. Z. God doesn't want me to listen to evil." His voice drifted off.

He looked like the same young man I had met with two weeks earlier. Or did he? Midnight hair. Hazel eyes. Coffee bean complexion. Yet a corpse-like pallor colored his cheeks, and his orange uniform hung off what was once his stocky yet muscular frame. He looked like he had lost a lot of weight.

"Have you been in the infirmary, Rudy? I haven't seen you up in school?"

Plus we'd been closed for a week.

"No, Ad Seg. I got into a fight in the middle of the vacation. I'm not going to listen to evil anymore."

Ad Seg—assigned segregation—code for solitary, meaning all the same.

The perils of time off. For us, the perks. For them, the perilous consequences. Ad Seg.

Too much time on their hands. For us, not enough.

For the minors, here, at least, lockdown, twenty hours a day. No school, no place to go. That's an awful lot of pent up energy and testosterone being locked up, waiting to explode. Like a nuclear reactor. A Chernobyl. Those cell doors open and whatever sideways conversations shared, hurled, cursed, argued, or confided, are resolved. The only way they know how. They know very little about conflict resolution. They only know how to use their fists.

Robert Listenbee, Jr. the administrator of the Office of Juvenile Justice and Delinquency Prevention, knows all about kids like Rodolfo—he knows that adolescents can be defiant and can hurt themselves and others, but he thinks that there might be other ways to treat young adults like Rodolfo, as opposed to how solitary is used with the adults. Makes sense, but it's probably expensive, and "more expensive" generally is a problem with reform. He agrees that sometimes there's no other way to deal with behavioral problems in jail other than separating the inmate from others, but he thinks that, for youthful offenders, that might be achieved without the isolation of Ad Seg.

Even for the older boys, who are lucky enough not to be locked in, time without school—that lack of purpose, that lack of schedule—leads to trouble.

No school. More time on their hands. More contact with each other. More contact with the COs. Either way, it can be a lethal combination.

You take a kid who has oppositional-defiant disorder (yes, there is such a thing—and it's not called stubborn) and you put him together with a scared new CO, and sparks fly.

I've been a very young new teacher who was instructed not to smile before Christmas; I don't know what instructions very young (sometimes twenty-one year old) COs are given, but I do know that there have been some pretty heated showdowns and trips to Ad Seg. Or even worse BMU where inmates are placed in *Plexiglas* cells with only air holes, and are muzzled with a spit mask and shackled just to go to the shower. Not a pretty sight to behold. Especially for a seventeen-year-old who has decided to spit at a CO who's pissed him off. Odds are, after BMU, he's never going to spit again.

I can't judge how things work. I don't live with the threat of serious injuries that the COs do. I do know human nature, though, and how things get bent out of shape when emotions are riding high. Emotions are pretty spent around here all the time. The COs are stressed, the inmates are stressed, and situations get stressed pretty quickly.

For Rodolfo, like most of the rest of our students, time without school, without a schedule, without anything to occupy the mind, equated to fights, and fights and more fights. In jail, when there's little else to do, there's always a fight.

When you're sixteen or seventeen or eighteen, there's always somebody to argue with. There's always something to argue about.

And when you're locked in all day and you have no place to go and the cage is open, and you're bursting to get out, and you're sixteen or seventeen or eighteen, you're almost guaranteed to get into some kind of fight.

And when you've got sixteen- or seventeen- or eighteen-year-old energy, and no place for it to go, and you're bursting to get out, and you're locked in all day, and you get into some kind of fight. Ad Seg.

Ad Seg—now, there's nobody to fight with. There's no one to argue with. And there's nothing, absolutely nothing, to do. No books. No TV. No radio. There's nothing but you and the four cell walls. There's nothing allowed. There's nothing. Nothing. There's nothing between you and your going crazy. Except—except the Bible.

The Bible. Your only companion.

And it's pretty damn lonely in there. Quiet. Nobody to talk to but yourself. And sometimes, you come out talking to Jesus. And sometimes, like Rodolfo, the devil.

"Living in a black hole"
—prison slang for solitary confinement

Chapter 16

Lockdowns

I don't know what it would be to like to be locked up in Ad Seg like Rodolfo. I've never really seen the inside of the cells used for solitary, but I do see the aftereffects. The cell study teachers, the ones who visit the boys locked in and bring them work, have described Ad Seg and BMU cells to me. Those teachers aren't allowed to visit the boys when they're assigned to either of those units, but they pass by them. You can't see in those cells; the doors don't permit any natural light. But sometimes the teachers stand outside and talk through the pocket door, or the CO opens the door a crack. The only access to the outside is the food tray pocket that's opened and closed, and there's only a mattress on the floor. The boys aren't allowed books or schoolwork. Only a Bible, or I imagine a Koran, something that will let you talk to God. Nothing else. Except you.

For the boys assigned to Ad Seg, you hope that they'll eventually come back to school. Many of them don't, and I'll never see them again. I never know what happens to them from then on. Some of them do, but, like Rodolfo, you notice the difference. Boys who were once sharp and clever, quick-witted lads, perhaps a bit too snappy and slick, return almost sluggish, slow on the uptake, too compliant and tired to explore the universe once so open to them. Like Rodolfo, there are dramatic changes. The way they talk, the way they walk, the way they look at you—so broken and so tamed. You actually wish for a cutting remark, a fast, intelligent comeback that screams, "Got ya!" and how you wish to hear them laugh. But they are absent any laughs for a long time afterward.

And they're thinner—dramatically so. I've had students who have lost as much as thirty pounds. A week or two of "cabbage loaf," our jail's nickname for jail and prison standard issue, *Nutraloaf*, will do that. *Nutraloaf* is a food served in US prisons to inmates in Ad Seg with just enough nutrition to sustain a prisoner; it is bland, intentionally unpleasant, and requires no utensils. Ad Seg prisoners are forced to eat with their hands. I'm not sure of Rodolfo's infraction, but I do know he's eighteen, and he hasn't been convicted of anything, only accused. Nobody knows if he's innocent or guilty yet.

I never really know if the punishment fits the crime. Ad Seg is delivered discriminately—a grievous assault, a cut or a cutting remark, or concealed contraband, a knife or a bag of tortilla chips. There are no standard lists of infractions for Ad Seg. How and when it is assigned is determined by individual COs; there is no quick appeal.

I just wish I could send my books. If I could only send my books, then maybe they'd have some company. Even if the jail screened them, that would be okay by me. If I could send anything.

Personally, I'd pick something funny, something

that might allow a laugh. And then, maybe something inspirational. I know that one of the more popular books that we had was Jack Canfield's *Chicken Soup for the Prisoner's Soul*. It didn't last long on the cart—a true sign of a book's success here, but a perfect choice for Ad Seg.

I remember listening to an *NPR* interview with a biographer of Nelson Mandela who wrote about what Mandela's reading selections were while on Robben Island, and how they changed him. Mandela was arrested as a political prisoner espousing the overthrow of government, the use of violence, and promoting a hatred for whites in South Africa. He emerged a political leader attempting to change his government and unite his country. Mandela said, "I came out mature." During that time, his maturity was developed by reading his enemy's mind, Afrikaner poetry and Afrikaner history, and changing his own. He shared Shakespeare's complete plays with his fellow inmates. That really makes me think about what it would mean to give those boys books while they're confined in those little cells.

There is an endless in and out to Ad Seg. It is not as uncommon as one might think, in the last five years.Over 90,000 juveniles have been held in solitary confinement in a jail, a prison or a juvenile facility in the United States.

Almost every day that I get my daily list, there are one or two boys who are no longer coming to school because they're locked up in Ad Seg—quite often for a long time. Young minds sit idle without mental stimulation, without social interaction and without emotional support. The United Nations Special Rapporteur on Torture condemned the use of solitary confinement for children as a violation of the prohibition against "cruel, inhuman, and degrading treatment," banned under several human rights treaties. Human Rights Watch published an entire report in October 2012, *Growing Up Locked Down*, specifically about juveniles locked up in the United States. Their conclusion: we need to stop. Yet our boys are still locked up. So are boys in most state jails and prisons. Ad Seg, unfortunately, is pretty much standard operating procedure in order to separate inmates from one another, so they don't hurt others, or hurt themselves, or to set an examples for others.

I can't see how locking up young men, depriving them of education or access to reading or self-improvement is going to help them learn anything. This isn't "Pelican Bay," a California maximum security prison synonymous with solitary confinement, where half of the prisoners are put in Ad Seg for management issues. Most of our students are going home and are going to try to make it in society again. I'd hope that improving their chances of getting a job or reading more might make them better citizens than they had been.

I was surprised to find out that the whole idea of Ad Seg was rejected by New York State back in the early 1800s when they were first building prisons. Too bad for Rodolfo that he wasn't incarcerated around then. Both New York and Pennsylvania wanted to provide a model for the rest of the country, and decided that adding monastic conditions to the accepted forced labor practices would improve prisoners' chances for rehabilitation. I don't think that Rodolfo found his experience to be the least bit monastic, despite the conversations that he's reported to have had with God.

So when the two states constructed a model, Pennsylvania opted for inmates to work, sleep, and eat in solitary cells—pretty close to Ad Seg—whereas New York favored inmates sleeping in separate cells but joining in a communal room for work and meals. The latter was called the Auburn System, where the first New York prison was built. Most other states adopted that system, too, simply because it was cheaper, not more spiritual. I suspect the current model might be cheaper, too.

I came to school this morning and got my daily list. Diquan was put in Ad Seg last night. I don't know what for, nor do I have the right to ask—one of the other boys will tell me later. He seems too small and scrawny to get in a fight, but the way he's been feeling lately, who knows what might make him explode? And who knows how sitting in the dark all by himself is going to make him feel?

"That's the thing about books. They let you travel without moving your feet."
—Jhumpa Lahiri, *The Namesake*

Chapter 17

Kris

"Can you leave a book for me tomorrow night?" Kris asks.

It's one of those rare instances when I'm back in the classroom, once my daily routine for twenty years, and now, a biweekly occurrence, night school.

Once our students get their GED, they move on to night school. Technically, they'd still be eligible to get their high school diplomas if they returned to their home districts, so we can address their educational needs until they're twenty-one. But we still need to free up space for new "applicants," and most of our guys don't want to leave. So, night school is our best option. You can come to school four nights—after dinner, 5 p.m. to 8 p.m., for two to three hours.

"Do you want a specific book, Kris?"

"No, you pick. Something interesting though." And he adds, "not too easy."

Kris doesn't need easy. He's bright, intelligent. Passed the GED with some of the highest scores we've seen. Besides that, he's witty and personable. The kind of kid that in some high school classes would have that edge, being able to engage adults more easily than the less sophisticated kids. He makes me laugh.

He comes to class and talks and talks. He talks about politics and current events and sports and the local news. If he could get his hands on a newspaper down on his house, his section of the jail, he'd have it read cover to cover. But newspapers are a commodity here, one more thing on the contraband list, one more seemingly innocuous thing that when soaked and hardened can become a weapon— something to be exchanged for services or other things, toothbrushes, approved prestamped envelopes, commissary-bought snacks, or hoarded food.

Interestingly, food is one of the most popular topics when the boys get together. Or they talk about the lack of it. Adolescent boys eat a lot. Having raised two, I know that gallons of milk disappear. I've seen a quart of milk sans glass downed in one sweep directly from the refrigerator. Despite, I'm sure, the adherence to nutritional guidelines, the guys here walk around hungry most of the time. Besides, there really aren't any true nutritional guidelines, anyway. There are no laws to regulate prison food; wardens and sheriffs determine food standards. The FDA monitors food quality and food production in the US, but those standards and health requirements do not extend to Prison Food Law. If the food's good, it's a courtesy extended, or it's from fear of a prisoner revolt. And it's happened at different places and different times, again. Food is an important issue.

So it shouldn't have surprised me when the book, *The Most Disgusting Food Sandwiches*, hit our top ten list. Yes, it was on the ALA Recommended List for Reluctant Readers, but when the book order arrived, and I saw this collection of photographs of oddly assembled sandwich combinations—*Krispy Kreme* donut buns with hamburgers and cheese in between—I couldn't have imagined its popularity. Our students would go from page to page to page, examining each oddball sandwich combination, the Garbage Food Parfait, the Macaroni and Cheese Bake, and probably imagine eating them. I don't know how filling imaginary eating might be, but this book filled their interest level and time.

This evening, Kris is chatting as usual with me in night school. He's asking me to leave a book for him when he comes up for school tomorrow night. He's talking about the upcoming presidential election, and then shifts to the local news. And then the subject of food comes up.

Like the rest of the boys, he's complaining to me about how small the portions are, and how he doesn't get enough to eat.

"I swear, Mrs. Z," he smiles. "If you gave me a can of Pedigree dog food right now, I'd eat it."

He laughs. I laugh. His sarcasm is meant to be funny. He knows how to be funny. He knows how to be funny even when the situation is not.

But my laughter haunts me later as I drive home. The rules dictate that I couldn't even give my students a candy cane at Christmas. My job here is far different from my role as teacher in the high school I came from. Sometimes, it's damn hard to downshift.

I know that according to the National Institutes of Health, a somewhat active fourteen- to eighteen-year-old needs between 2,400 to 2,800 calories a day. Increase that to very active and they'll need close to 3,200.

I honestly don't know how many calories they get

each day. In prisons and jails that post their menus (yes, there are some), the average daily menu has about 2,000 to 2,400 calories. I do know that they are not adjusting these menus for size or age.

I don't know if there is a nutritionist on staff. I do know that I have a friend who is a dietician, and she goes crazy when she finds out that a nursing home or a school cafeteria isn't staffed by a certified dietician. When I questioned her about whether or not she thought the jail had one, she didn't seem as concerned.

Whether Kris eats *Pedigree* dog food or not, doesn't concern most people. He's a kid, and he's been arrested. Guilty. As far as most people are concerned, Kris is being fed at taxpayer's expense, and he's getting more than bread and water. I don't know if his nutritional needs are being met. What growing teenage boys need and what a thirty-year-old man needs nutritionally are very different. Prison menus don't adjust for these discrepancies. My friend would be the first to tell you that.

My area of expertise is not nutrition, nor am I as creative a cook as some of these guys. A commissary pop tart is heated in the clothes dryer, Fritos corn chips and spicy Cheetos inside a plastic bag mixed with hot water and set to harden become prison tamales. I discovered that Martha Stewart created crab apple jelly during her stay at Alderson Federal Prison, but with less creativity—she had access to a kitchen, and the COs reportedly looked the other way when she did her apple picking. Piper Kerman, author of the popular *Orange Is The New Black*, gives a recipe for prison cheesecake made with graham crackers, lemon juice, vanilla pudding mix, stolen margarine, and coffee creamer.

Yes, in jail, hunger trumps necessity as the mother of all invention.

So Kris is hungry a lot of the time. I realize I can't possibly assuage his hunger pains. The only appetite I can satisfy with Kris is the one he has for reading.

That book of odd sandwiches did the same thing. Those sandwiches weren't real, but they did feed those boys' imaginations—an organ that is as hungry as their stomachs are.

"We all are men, in our own natures frail, and capable of our flesh; few are angels."
—William Shakespeare, *Henry VIII*

Chapter 18

No Visitors Today

Most metro libraries have bilingual collections. English and Spanish are obvious. But in places like New York City, Farsi or Tagalog or Russian line the shelves. Our library is lucky it has a few good *libros* on its cart. And I'm happy it does.

I'm leaving school earlier than usual because they've had a lockdown; the entire jail's locked in. Good news, nothing bad's happened: no inmate fights, no COs hurt. The radio system's down and security is compromised. For me, a few more minutes to run errands. For the boys, extra hours shut in today.

I was late coming back from lunch and parked in the visitors' lot instead of the back. Now it's unusually busy. They've cleared the visitors' room because of the radio failure. "Everyone, go home." And everyone is going home—all at once. It happens randomly, but often enough. Doesn't matter how far you've come; doesn't matter who you've come to see.

"But my husband's being sent upstate tomorrow."

"Sorry, ma'am. No visitors today."

Babies wail. Grandmothers push walkers back to their cars. Bent and tired mothers make their way out of the parking lot and cross the street toward the bus stop.

"No visitors today." No matter how far you've come or how long you've waited.

I'm opening my car door, and a woman in the car next to me rolls down her window. "Is everything all right in there? I'm here almost every day, and I know when they lock down that someone gets hurt. These guys are like my babies."

I know how she feels. I do recognize her from the lobby every day as I walk back from lunch. "No, no. Nothing like that. A technical problem. That's what I was told. I work in the school. What do you do here?"

"I'm an interpreter for the lawyers who come to visit."

In New York, that's almost two and a half million New Yorkers who need her services. There are that many New Yorkers who do not speak English and have a limited ability to read, speak, write, or understand English. That's the tricky part when deciding when to give one of our guys an interpreter—knowing what they can and can't do in English.

Since I had taught ESL for so many years, I already know: You can talk a good game, take part in pretty ordinary conversations, and talk about last night's reality TV series, but it doesn't mean you're proficient in English. When you go to court, you need to be able to read the documents you sign, understand what you've read, and understand what your lawyer or interpreter is explaining to you. Over 11 percent of Nassau County's residents speak English less than "very well." Add to that, all those guys I see who have fallen "under the radar" and haven't been counted in those statistics—I'd say there are a few percentage points more.

That's a lot of people needing interpreter services, and there is a huge difference between a translator and an interpreter. Interpreting is a lot more difficult than translating. It means much more than just knowing another language; it means understanding the legal jargon in both languages, understanding the nuances of the legal system, and understanding the proficiency level of the individual that you're interpreting for. If I was working with a Hector, I would be explaining things in Spanish a lot differently than I would to a Rodolfo, who had just emerged all jumbled and confused from Ad Seg.

Being an interpreter is a far more complex task. Right now the New York State United Court System offers interpreter services in Albanian; Arabic; Bengali; BCS-Bosnian/Croatian/Serbian; Cantonese; French; Greek; Haitian Creole; Hebrew; Hindi; Italian; Japanese; Korean; Mandarin; Polish; Portuguese; Punjabi; Russian; Spanish; Urdu; Vietnamese; and Wolof, the language spoken in Senegal. There are no minimum educational qualifications to be one, just a test of oral proficiency and writing. I don't know if I'd want the outcome of my legal case dependent on someone who might do just fine on a test in their native language, but has never set foot in an arraignment court.

"*Me mucho gusta.*" I muster up the best Spanish I can, expressing how pleased I am to meet her. Of course, that's where our Spanish conversation ends.

"Nice to meet you, too." She laughs. And corrects my Spanish, "It's *mucho gustO*. I'm Maritza, by the way."

"*Gracias. Mucho gusto,*" and I shake her hand.

She's right, of course. Usually, when there's a lockdown, something has gone wrong. There has been a fight. Someone has been hurt. Inmate or CO. It's nothing funny. Serious stuff.

Maritza might have told me, *Hierba mala nunca muere.* (Weeds never die.) Although my Spanish is terrible now, it used to be pretty good when I was living in Argentina for a while.

This morning, there was a fight in school. Only the fourth one I've seen in four years. One in four. Pretty low stats. For me. But there's plenty that I never see. For the COs, the stakes are very high.

Two COs got hurt—bruises and sprains. At least five students have some kind of black eye or bruise. One student is now in Ad Seg. And who knows what started the whole thing?

But this is reality. You can't talk about jail or prison without mentioning it. This isn't an orphanage. Or Boys Town. You don't see Mickey Rooney, not that anyone would even know who Mickey Rooney would be, carrying a skinny little boy in the rain for miles and shouting, "He ain't heavy, Fa'dah, he's my brot'er."

It doesn't matter where these boys come from. What their stories are. If they are innocent or guilty. It doesn't matter where the COs come from. What their stories are. It doesn't matter what's mine. Or my coworkers'. Or the medical staff's.

We're all locked in a very dark and dangerous place for at least part of our day.

For some of us, the danger is very close at hand. For

some, it is rare. But Maritza's right, there's good reason for lockdowns.

When sparks go flying, everything shuts down, before something really ignites.

After witnessing the few fights that I have (and I thank God I've only seen the few), I have nothing but pure respect for the COs who work here. Stereotyped or not— *Cool Hand Luke* be damned—these guys' lives are put on the lines when all hell breaks loose. And they step up to the plate. They act as a team and secure order for both the other inmates and themselves.

And those COs have good reason to want things secure. In 2011, correction officer was ranked in the top five occupations with the highest number of non-fatal occupational injury or illness days away from work, five times greater than the national average.

I'm sitting across the desk from Benjamin. His face is swollen, and it is obvious someone's jumped him from behind.

"And the CO got us both against the wall," he grumbles, "and then frisked us down." He's furious. As furious as only the innocent can be. I can't blame him. But I can't blame the CO, either. It wasn't up to him to decide who was guilty or who was innocent—both inmates were in a fight.

They found a shank taped to the inside calf of one of our quietest students when they frisked him. Shanks, homemade weapons made from an assortment of readily found items, come in all shapes and sizes—toothbrushes, sharpened eating utensils, papier-mâché toilet paper spears, disassembled table parts, can become "weapons of opportunity." A nearby broom handle or dustpan—what seems innocuous to you or me—can be lethal. And there is a list of other contraband items, too, that seem less dangerous, but when used as a means of extortion or manipulation or gang recruitment are quite as powerful, too: betting slips, or candy, the basic ingredient for any good hooch, a prison-made alcohol drink made from anything that can ferment. Then there are the more recent additions: tattoo guns, branding gang members their allegiances. Inmates pass kites, an intra-jail messaging system which contain any one of many master plans. What might seem harmless enough—a stick of chewing gum—will turn what is supposed to be a closed entry into an open access when plugging a lock. So, I shouldn't be surprised when Benjamin tells me about Pedro and the shank discovered taped to his leg. But I am.

"Not Pedro. You gotta be kidding."

One of the COs reminds me: "Who they are with you isn't how they act on the tier. You gotta remember how they might react all of the time."

It is a reminder that the COs never forget: anyone, anywhere inside, can be a threat.

I often walk into work with the COs in the morning. These guys (and women) often grumble on their way in, "One more day until I retire," or "Another day in hell," or something just as negative. At first, I was quite judgmental about their comments. I kept thinking that a job is as positive as the energy you bring to it. No wonder they're so unhappy about what they do. Well, I felt that way until I understood the daily stress the COs work with—of never knowing who might be concealing a weapon, of who might start a fight, of who might have a psychotic episode, of who might prevent you from simply going home at the end of the day. Then my opinion changed. My opinion has changed about a lot of things since I've got here.

"Weeds never die" (*Hierba mala nunca muere*). And some weeds look just like flowers. Only the experienced gardener distinguishes what to pull and what to nurture.

With Pedro, I suspect that shank wasn't meant to hurt anyone. It was a means of self-protection. But that CO was right: you can't walk toward a man sure his gun's unloaded unless you're the one who has unloaded it.

I try to remind Benjamin of this. He concedes.

All I know is that it is a lot easier watching some program about jail on TV than it is working in one. Being in jail stinks no matter which side of the bars you sit on.

"We owe it to each other to tell stories."
—Neil Gaiman, *Coraline*

Chapter 19

David's Secret

They say that art imitates life. It's awfully difficult to imitate an adolescent's or young adult's life. Even harder to imitate a young inmate's.

Yet many have tried. Young adult literature. Young adult fiction. They even have young adult librarians, specialists in the mysterious young adult's mind that so few want to venture in or return to.

At first glance, it's doubtful that our students would have anything to do with young adult. They don't fit the image of the kid at the library in the Teen Club. Most of them had simply been riding the cusp of young adulthood anyway. Pushing past the library card definition, anyway. In fact, most of them probably had never had a library card to get into the children's section, let alone the young adult one. As if swept by a wave, they had ridden over childhood too fast. It had been a bumpy ride.

Our little library—yes, a collection of books that circulate can be defined as one—offers these boys an opportunity to form their own Teen Club of sorts. Before their arrests, they were a group that largely wasn't served by their community libraries, which usually jumped in on the school-to-jail pipeline—discouraging their participation in them, and using the same punitive and isolating responses that their schools did to keep them out. The library simply wasn't an inviting place; the streets were.

But there's a reason public libraries are so keen on Teen Clubs: they can help guide teens through a very tumultuous period of human growth and development. Reading and reflecting on what's been read are important components in a teenager's growth and development, in shaping the adult personality, in embracing values. For the first time in their lives, our students may be removed from the distractions that kept them from reading when there is little else to do, and then, they read. Our little library is a lot more important than the boys just borrowing paperbacks off a cart.

Devon had rushed the cart as soon as I rolled into his classroom. "Mrs. Z, do you have Harry Potter number five?"

Devon had been rifling through the remnants of the book cart. It looked skeletal after Christmas break. And I hadn't had time to beef it up with any returns.

Harry Potter had come and gone as a jail bestseller a couple of sentences ago. I only had a couple of volumes left on the cart, although I had almost a complete set in Spanish.

"I probably could find it, Devon. Have you read the other four?"

Devon nodded. He almost looked embarrassed to ask until Santos boastfully added, "I've read all seven, Mrs. Z." Two felons, an attempted assault and a robbery, were escaping to Hogwarts School of Witchcraft and Wizardry and were reading young adult literature. Oddly, when they were no longer given the safety of being young.

But I've suspected for a long time that most of these guys were never given the safety of being young, the protection afforded the innocent or the ignorance given the naive. They were adults well before finishing childhood.

I eyed David in the corner of the room. There he was—always the child, lowering himself in his chair and becoming smaller and smaller despite his length of limb. It always amazed me how small he could become.

I asked to speak to him just to check in. David wasn't someone I could easily ignore. I'd speak with him almost every day, but it had been a while since we had really talked.

We walked across the hall. "You want to know a secret, Mrs. Z?"

I really didn't. TMI. Too much information. Just like the guys, I'd learned that I didn't want to know some things. What I didn't know, I didn't need to report. I wasn't sure what kind of secret David wanted to tell.

But David persisted. He bent forward, lifted his head, opened one eye, and squinted at me. "My mother can't work."

This didn't seem much like a secret. I understood that she was disabled.

David continued, "because she's always on the computer. I swear to God, Mrs. Z, she's on the computer as we speak." He paused and seemed to reflect on the irony. "And it's messed her up so much—she can't work."

It was confusing to me. I didn't get it.

"You know those little cartoon people you can get on the computer, Mrs. Z? You can dress 'em up and go on the computer and talk to other people with 'em."

"You mean avatars?"

"Yeah, yeah, avatars. That's what I mean, Mrs. Z. My mom, she got one of those avatars and we gave her some money for it. She bought her avatar things—clothes, and bling, and all kinds of stuff—and started going on the computer with it. Then she borrowed my sister's credit card. She was spending all her money on the computer. And then all her time." David paused. He thought about it before he continued as if he was still trying to figure it all out. "And then she couldn't go to work." And then the little boy sat up.

"It sounds like she's very unhappy, David."

He nodded. He looked across the desk, relieved that I hadn't said she was crazy. Relieved that I had said "unhappy." Relieved. Relieved that I hadn't said, lazy, deadbeat. All words he had heard before. I said "unhappy." And David was relieved.

"You know, Mrs. Z. Now that I got my GED, when I get out o' here, I'm going to buy my mother all of those things she's been buying her avatar. I'm going to try to make my mother happy."

And I thought about David and his mom and the little cartoon person. It could be any person, or anything, or any drug. Sometimes being young gets cut short. And there are a lot of ways to get out of ourselves.

"David, I know you'll make your mother happy. You're a very thoughtful young man." I know he'd try. He probably always had.

David gushed. He laughed nervously. Compliments made him uncomfortable. And silence made him anxious.

"And ya know, about sending my GED, Mrs. Z." He cleared his throat. "Hmm, can you make me some copies when the certificate comes in, 'cause I'm still not sure if the address I put down is where my mother lives. My phone account went dead, and I can't get her or my sister. I ain't talked to nobody in my family lately."

"No problem," I assured him. "Did you talk to your lawyer about when he thinks you're being released? Are you being released?" It was clear that David was facing double the challenge of getting out—what to do and where to live.

"Nah, but I hope maybe another month or two. He said I could get county time." At least that would buy us some time.

David browsed the shelves on the cart before he left. "What's this one about?" he asked, holding up a copy of *Rikers High*.

"Oh, it's about boys attending high school on Rikers Island."

He put the book back on the shelf.

"I've gotten some good reviews on it." Always trying to negotiate the sell.

David glanced back at me from his bent frame and grinned. "Mrs. Z, why would I want to read a book about a bunch of guys like me? I'm already sitting in jail. I try to read something that helps me escape."

I laughed. To each our own escape.

Wisdom punches you right in the gut sometimes. Knocks the wind out of you when it comes out of nowhere, well, out of where you least expect it.

I wish I could give David more choices of books that offered him the opportunity for escape. I know that there are lists and lists of books that these boys could relate to—books relevant to their lives and experiences. There are specific groups such as Library Services for Youth in Custody posted by the Colorado State Library website who have created specific book lists and even a book award for incarcerated youth. There are books better suited for some of their reading abilities. We have one small cart, a small budget, and the large hearts of a small group of donors. Our books don't necessarily fit the description of culturally relevant. However, our books, as David insisted, allow for escape or for personal transformation. For some of the boys, books like *Rikers High* not only described their life experience but also gave them someone to identify with, a someone who had been in jail and tried to change. For others, like David, *Harry Potter and the Sorcerer's Stone* allowed him escape and recreation, time to decompress and relieve the stress of being in jail. Either way, libraries in jail give students the opportunity to go beyond their own experiences and get out, or to think about ways they might get out. Simply put, our library, like the public library they should have been visiting on the outside, could give these guys an opportunity to grow, to escape, and, most of all— to change.

David's mother's avatar. Harry Potter's fellow muggles. Rick Riordan's mythical fantasies. The chance for escape— to another place, to someone else's life, to an earlier time. That was David's. For other boys, real. For some, mystery. Others, vampires.

Art does imitate life. But not always our own. Purposely so. Sometimes, we seek to imitate lives unknown, undiscovered, unrealized.

Books, the chance for art to weave the stories about lives, about characters, about themes and plots and conflicts, sometimes similar to our own, sometimes not. And then there are the stories so real, so starkly real, so brutally honest, they seem like our own.

Stories like David's. And all the others I listen to. Their wisdom can sneak right up on you and punch you right in the gut. Not a lot of people here notice them. If they did, they'd knock the wind right out of them.

"One's dignity may be assaulted, vandalized and cruelly mocked, but it can never be taken away unless it is surrendered."
—Michael J. Fox

Chapter 20

Rasheed and Isaiah

Did anybody bring any Stuart Woods back, Mrs. Z?"

"No, we're all out of Stuart Woods, Isaiah."

There were only two students in classroom 2 this afternoon, both prepping for the GED, but eager to bring books back to their cells.

Rasheed scolded me for bringing the cart to them last. "If you had brought us the cart before the other rooms, there'd be some Stuart Woods left."

I let him scold. Rasheed usually just scowled. His long angular face descended with each cynical remark and rose with each target assaulted. Despite his permanent frown, he was a handsome young man—tall, cocoa beige, long dreads, and lean. His good looks were going to waste in here.

For the record, Rasheed doesn't like me. Well, he didn't like me.

Over the last few months, little by slowly, I'd been softening him. I could feel it more than see it. He still scowled. He didn't smile. But I could see that the fighter in him had left the ring.

Rasheed, along with a lot of the other boys, comes in here feeling cheated. Whatever they were supposed to have had in life they didn't get, so that they are ready to fight for whatever they have left. Most of the time, just their dignity.

Dignity is a pretty precious thing to protect. Pretty rare, too. And Rasheed knew it. When I met him, I saw a lot of it in him and knew not to take it. We got along after that.

Not everyone operates on that theory. The other inmates. Some of the COs. They're ready to take the little dignity you have left and beat it right out of you. And then, you're left with nothing.

You can get jumped for a lot of things in here. Sometimes, I get all bent out of shape because my books don't come back. I go in and out of the classrooms and read aloud names and remind them of books they need to bring back. This collection of burglars and car thieves and sometimes murderers makes up the same kind of flimsy excuses that an unsophisticated fourth grader might—"I forgot it, I'll bring it tomorrow ... The CO took it from me ... I lent it to ...," and so on and so on. I forget that these boys get jumped for books, for food, for the smallest of sundry items—even a postage stamp. They get jumped just for being who they are. And then they've taken everything. I forget about that.

Rasheed held onto his dignity tightly. I admired that. It looked as if he owned nothing when he possessed everything. Because of that, he wanted for nothing.

Isaiah interrupted. "You know it's my twenty-first birthday today, Mrs. Z," he said proudly.

"A man."

I looked at him and Rasheed and thought about their becoming men. About the gaps in this becoming. The times in juvenile centers. Their stays in jail. Those gaps. The things not in their life that are supposed to help the child grow.

"Happy Birthday, Isaiah." I smiled. "Why don't you take this book to read?" I handed him a copy of *Black Profiles in Courage* by Kareem Abdul-Jabbar. "Read something besides Stuart Woods."

Isaiah shook his head. He only knew to choose one kind of book—much the way that he only knew to choose one way of life.

I kept nudging him. "How bad could it be? Take the book back to your cell. If you don't like it, bring it back to me tomorrow."

I wish someone had kept nudging him—to stay in school, to stay off the streets, to pay attention, to …

But then, nobody had. And now, things were different. They were becoming men without seeing the choices they had. Isaiah was turning twenty-one without a party, and Rasheed wasn't going to celebrate one.

They got up to go. They didn't look like men. Their orange pants hung down as far as any banger on the street. The gloved COs waited in the hallway to pat them down as they swaggered rather than walked toward the door. But before he left, Rasheed turned to remind me, "Make sure we're first tomorrow, Mrs. Z—you promised."

I'd make sure of it. He'd already had too many broken promises in his lifetime. Promising him a book wasn't offering him much.

"The greater ignorance towards a country is not ignoring what its politicians have to say, it is ignoring what the inmates in its prisons have to say."
—Criss Jami, *Venus In Arms*

Chapter 21

Ishmel Is Free to Read

Libraries are founded on the whole idea of intellectual freedom—that everyone has the right to pursue knowledge, to explore ideas. In other words, to find out the truth for themselves.

So if I want to read about Karl Marx, then I should be allowed to read about Karl Marx. Joe McCarthy be damned.

The American Library Association takes this very seriously and defends this right—standing up for it whenever it's challenged. And in theory, at least, that right extends to jails—every prisoner has the right to read whatever they want. In theory. But rarely, at least, in practice. And every prisoner has even more reason to read.

Supreme Court Justice Thurgood Marshall wrote in *Procunier v Martinez* [416 US 428 (1974):

> When the prison gates slam behind an inmate, he does not lose his human quality; his mind does not become closed to ideas; his intellect does not cease to feed on a free and open interchange of opinions; his yearning for self-

respect does not end; nor is his quest for self-realization concluded. If anything, the needs for identity and self-respect are more compelling in the dehumanizing prison environment.

And if history proves anything, we read story after story of men and women who transformed the world with books written in prison, St. Paul, probably being the earliest, and Dr. Martin Luther King Jr. in *Letters from a Birmingham Jail.*

I know that one of the more popular books to walk lately would be sitting under the censor microscope if anyone cared to notice. But no one has but the students.

"Do you have any more copies of *Behold a Pale Horse*, Mrs. Z?" Ishmel asks eagerly.

"I do, in the cabinet. That seems to be on the top ten list."

After retrieving it, I quip, "Are you really going to read this? I couldn't plow through this in a million years."

The book is thick. The font size smaller. It is full of maps and graphs and detailed illustrations and charts. Not easy to digest.

"You planning on becoming an anarchist?" I ask.

His answer leaves little cause for concern. "What's an anarchist?"

Ishmel is free to find out. He is free to decide whether there mightn't be a better design for government than the one we have. He is free to find out if the system of "you're innocent until you're proven guilty" is the most workable or is there a more workable one.

For all I know, Ishmel might be one of those

individuals who writes a book. From prison. Who might transform the world. Like Henry David Thoreau, who also spent time in jail and concluded that "Things do not change. We change."

And Ishmel is still young enough to.

The American Library Association believes Ishmel can change, and that what he reads might change him. It believes that his freedom to choose what he reads will help him change. They set forth their statement, *Prisoners' Right to Read, An Interpretation of the Library Bill of Rights*, in order that he might be able to have the right to read.

The ALA takes this right seriously and goes to great lengths to defend it for everyone, prisoners like Ishmel included. And for the boys who get old in jail, they still get the chance to change, too—when they can choose what they want to read.

Ishmel is lucky—he'll probably only serve eighteen months.

"Part of being young is making mistakes."
—Nikki Reed

Chapter 22

Tyshana

I am the first to admit that the most frustrating part of this job is the not knowing—of the never knowing—what happens after the boys leave. I hate the transiency, how quickly some of these boys cross over my emotions and heart as if I were a stone amidst a running stream. The flip side of the frustration is the knowing—knowing if they come back. Seeing a boy's name on my morning list whom I had just seen two months before. Of seeing that boy's name three and four times in the course of a year. So, I'm damned if I do and damned if I don't—do I want to know what happens next, or don't I?

It's called recidivism—rooted in a Latin verb, *caedere*, meaning fall, and the prefix, *re,* go back—to fall back—which is not difficult to do once you're back out on the street and limited in what you can do.

As my worlds inside and outside of jail increasingly begin to intersect, I am reminded of this falling back in the oddest way.

My husband's home health aide arrives early one morning and chats over a cup of coffee. She proudly displays photos of her grandchildren on her iPhone and explains her court motion to gain custody of her granddaughter from her son.

My antennae heighten.

At first, her reasons are vague. She dances around it, almost feeling the temperature of the room—instead, talking about these kids in her neighborhood having kids and her section of South Queens being divided into two gangs: the part inhabited by the Bloods, the other, the Crips.

And I enter her conversation. "Believe it or not, I know about the Bloods and the Crips."

She looks at me with surprise and with attitude. As if I could hear her thinking, *What, did you read about them in a sociology class? Or go to the movies?*

"You know where I work?"

And I give her the opening to discover that her son has done time, a lot of it, and more than once. And that even with the birth of that adorable little girl whose photo I just saw on the iPhone, he's gone back on the street and is using again. He had a chance for a job and a scholarship to a business college and, as she explains with frustration, he had a chance to turn things around. But he didn't take it.

And our lives intertwine. I talk about my frustrations with the system. With my job. I talk about my frustration with a system that elects to incarcerate juveniles of fifteen or sixteen or seventeen for minor offenses, rather than seeking better alternatives—even with evidence from the 2010 Juvenile Justice Report that this approach results in a 89 percent reoffender rate for boys and 81 percent for girls. I think of the boys I interview who recite a litany of Juvenile Detention Center names as if offering benediction. Tyshana lists the JDCs her son has resided in. He's been in Rikers three times, and he's just turned twenty-one. Unlike forty-eight other states, New York treats sixteen- and seventeen-year-olds as adults, despite the research that yells that doing so accomplishes nothing other than producing future criminals. Tyshana and I talk about our frustrations with a system that expects kids carrying felonies on their backs at age seventeen or eighteen or twenty to find a future. I think about Dyshone back in Long Beach and Diquan who hasn't surfaced yet from Ad Seg. And we talk about probation, how easily these boys blow it. Within three years, more than 25 percent are back in jail again. I talk with her about a system that already knows that carrying a felony pretty much bars you from doing anything worthwhile. It pretty much puts you back behind bars, a different kind, and now without the taxpayers' expense. For a while. Because without a decent job or a decent education, you can pretty much expect nothing. And when you can pretty much expect nothing, then you can pretty much expect the kid to go back to doing nothing, to being nothing, and to expecting nothing good. And you can bet nothing good ever comes of it.

My husband's home health aide knows all about this. Firsthand. A lot of people only read about it in books.

"Jesus himself did not try to convert the two thieves on the cross; he waited until one of them turned to him."
—Dietrich Bonhoeffer, *Letters and Papers from Prison*

Chapter 23

Angelo

Some books don't fit on regular-size shelves. They're too wide, too long, or too heavy. They're shelved on shelves of their own.

I've found the same goes for people.

The boys would like me to believe that the COs are the enemy. They shelve everyone in a gray uniform here onto one big shelf. If the boys want everyone to be cataloged and Dewey Decimaled like that, then they'd all be shelved together, too. I don't think they'd like that.

It's good for library reference books, not for people.

People come in many different sizes. A lot of them can be shelved together, but then you get to the ones that are unique—not the same size as everybody else. They need their own special shelf. If I wanted to shelve everyone here in a gray uniform onto one shelf, then Angelo definitely couldn't fit—he'd have to have a shelf all his own.

As I wheel the cart down the hall to each classroom, I can't help but walk past Angelo a million times a day, back and forth in front of the desk where he sits sentry all day. Sometimes, we chat. Sometimes, we don't. Sometimes, we

131

just smile. Being sentry is really a very monotonous job—90 percent preparedness, 10 percent activity. It requires a lot of sitting around. But it's not boring. There's a lot of tension. Being on edge. Never knowing when the powder keg is going to explode. Sort of like working with a stick of dynamite strapped to your back. A good job description for an average CO. Angelo's earned his way to working up here in the school. On the tiers, the 90 percent formula drops significantly, to about 50 percent; and as it does, the stress level rises—a constant 100 percent. There are some days, you can feel the tension as you do humidity in the air. It is an odd kind of feel. But you sense a fight brewing or something going down without even knowing about it. And I'm only here a few hours a day.

I notice that Angelo wears a silver dinosaur pin on his pocket lapel.

"What's it mean, Angelo?"

"I'm old." He chuckles. "I'm almost extinct around here." Angelo's clocked in more than twenty years. Quite an achievement in a profession whose average life expectancy is about fifty-eight. That doesn't leave you a helluva lot of years in retirement.

Angelo, the dinosaur? Extinct? Certainly, distinct. Angelo sets a tone, and it is nothing but respectful.

He's here early—very early—and has his crew cleaning the school area, the bathrooms, our offices, the little kitchenette where we make lunch. So, most mornings, when I come off the elevator, I'm greeted by Angelo and an Orange Julius work crew mopping and sweeping the floors. The smell of Pine Sol, well a cheaper county contracted industrial solvent—fills the unventilated space we fondly call school.

"Okay, guys, why don't you get in here?" he suggests as he directs his crew.

"We gotta get some toilet paper rolls. Let's try and change the garbage bags over in that office. Watch your step, now, the floor is wet."

There are no commands with Angelo. No sharp edges. You wonder how he ever became a CO. How he ever became extinct. How he might have ever survived sitting watch over the turmoil of the tiers. But he has, and has emerged a soft and gentle man.

They're finished cleaning. Angelo pours them each a cup of coffee. A delicacy here. Coveted. And each man sits down on one of the plastic couches in our little kitchenette.

"Did you see what those Mets did last night? They creamed Detroit." One of the crew comments as if he had been at Citifield last night.

And one of our teachers starts to put in his two cents.

And I feel like I'm in a locker room. And those three inmates do, too. And we're all sitting and having our morning coffee. And for five or ten minutes, we're talking about last night's baseball. We're all sitting together and acting normal.

"Okay, guys, we have to get back," Angelo interrupts this illusion of normalcy and those guys throw out their cups, grateful for as simple a thing as conversation.

Angelo isn't really such an exception to the rule. There would be a lot of oversized books on that CO shelf. There are an awful lot of men and women like Angelo who come to work every day, want to earn a day's pay, and just go home every night. They want to keep it as safe a day as possible and go home and see their children after. They want to treat the people they meet fairly, whether inmate or coworker. They just want to be human.

Recently, one of the boys confided that the only thing that kept him sane his first month here was the CO on his tier who walked by every night and wished him a good night's sleep. Sounds like something out of a Hollywood movie script, but it's true and happens more often than you might think.

Angelo reminds me of Tom Hanks in "The Green Mile." Struggling to maintain human dignity and respect even in the despair of death row. Angelo does that here.

And the Angelos and the COs who wish a frightened sixteen-year-old a good night's sleep are the people who can make a difference in an inmate's life. Sometimes, instead of the reentry programs or the rehab programs or the writing programs or, yes, even the school programs or a rolling library. In the most dehumanizing place, they add the touch of humanity. Angelo probably doesn't even know he does that.

Whenever Angelo answers the phone or calls one of the other officers, he always ends the same: "Thanks, brother." Initially, I thought it funny—Angelo, obviously more an Italian stallion, didn't possess much soul. Over time, I've come to realize that the "brother" he refers to is the band of brothers that has formed between him and his fellow officers who will insure each other's safety, who watch each other's back.

Angelo hopes that there will never be an us against them. He doesn't see anyone belonging on one shelf or another. But he knows that if someone did, he'd be considered an enemy, no matter how many coffees he'd pour. That's jail reality.

In the meantime, Angelo and a lot of other COs think it's more important to be kind and human and respectful toward the inmates. It's more important not to have them feel less than. But always keeping up their guard. Never forgetting to keep up their guard.

"Behavior is a mirror in which everyone displays his own image."
—Johan Wolfgang Van Goethe

Chapter 24

Invictus

A lot of people would expect me to say that Angelo is a complete anomaly, the exception to the rule. They'd expect me to say that overall, I meet angry, belligerent and hostile COs. But that's not true. It's been just the opposite. TV, the movies and my students would like you to believe otherwise.

It's one of the stresses that COs suffer once they take the job—poor public image. They start out as simple civil servants, people looking for stable government jobs, with health benefits and a good retirement—not that much different from me. They end up working in a highly stressful environment, along with having a poor public image and receiving poor pay.

"The public hasn't a clue as to what correctional officers do. Someone asked me the other day if I beat inmates all day." That's what an officer told an interviewer preparing the National Institute of Justice's Report on Correctional Officer Stress. Add to this the starting average salary as reported by the Department of Labor Statistics in 2010, $39,020.

There are many people who view police officers as "cleaning up the streets," correction officers as "keeping a lid on" the refuse that's been collected. Police officers are highly respected, correction officers are not—by the public or by those they are in charge of. They can't win for trying—they get no respect. And they deserve some.

I don't envy any of them their jobs. I get to see kids exclusively for one thing—education, an inherently positive endeavor. If things get unmanageable, I don't really have to manage any of them. I have two COs in the hall to manage for me, when and if the students get out of hand. When people find out that I work in a jail, they don't ask me if I am beating my students. Generally, they are curious about what I do, what the students have done and if they will succeed. They look at what I am doing as something positive. I feel that I am doing something positive.

And there are plenty of COs who care—who wish that their job descriptions would go beyond "enforcing rules and regulations." The kids know who they are, and so do I. They stand out but don't get any credit for it. And, truthfully, a lot of them do. I see the COs who are assigned desk duty in the school and engage in conversations with the boys, who suggest paths that they might take when they get out. I've seen COs who on their own initiative have provided some level of guidance in helping some very illiterate inmates fill out legal documents. I've seen a CO set up a lending library with a self-designed computer catalog in the main law library—trust me, I was impressed. I see COs interact with inmate work crews and other COs who staff the visitor's reception room assist family members with what is otherwise a very lengthy and frustrating process.

I'm teaching night school and my lesson is on Nelson Mandela. I've decided to show the film, *Invictus*, with

Morgan Freeman and Matt Damon, which takes its name from a poem written by William Ernest Henley. The poem inspired Nelson Mandela while he was in prison. *Invictus*: Latin, for undefeated. The closing lines, "I am the master of my fate, I am the captain of my soul …" seem powerful lines to discuss with boys whose lives have yet to unfold and whose choices have taken them to jail. We discuss the title, and one of the boys quite insightfully explains that even when you're locked up in jail, no one can conquer your mind or your soul. That belongs to you, no matter what.

As part of the lesson, I've created a PowerPoint on Mandela's life, including photographs of the prison at Robben Island, his cell and the prison yard. I'm pointing out the size of his cell, the lack of toilet facilities, the work yard with boulders and stones, and the isolated position of the island in the middle of the ocean. The boys are very interested.

The classroom door opens, and Richie, the CO on duty tonight, pokes his head in the door. "Do you mind if I watch, too?" He comes in and stands next to me as I advance the slides and continue to discuss Mandela's life.

When we're finished and the boys are about to do their reading, Richie turns to leave but provides them with a lesson of his own, "Pay attention to the lesson, guys. You wanna get out of here, too, and do something useful with your life."

Thank you, Richie. I need all the reinforcement I can get. But most nights that I am teaching night school with Richie, I have reasons to thank him. He'll let a guy up late if he's had a visitor because he knows school's important. He'll just come in and chat. In here, the simplest of human gestures are appreciated. Richie is in a thankless job—no one recognizes his contributions to these human beings. He's continually up against working overtime, understaffing, and working different shifts. He's been hired to maintain order, check for contraband, make sure the inmates are accounted for. No one cares if he engages with them positively or not. He's added that on his own. He wants to help the guys who find themselves in jail to never come back, but the system doesn't help him do that. It's not set up that way.

Later that week, I'm on the Number 7 train headed to Manhattan, and the train stops in Long Island City, pretty close to Rikers Island, when two very tough and nefarious looking guys get on. You can feel the tension in the car rise dramatically. These two kids look threatening. One is dressed in camouflage, the other in clothes that clash intentionally, creating an aura of conflict around him. He has red-and-green plaid shorts dropped hip high and a black-and-blue Hawaiian floral shirt. What I can't miss are his very Kelly green sneakers—I don't know the brand or the name, but I know they are about status. They both look mean. As threatened as I feel, I can't help but laugh—I keep thinking that these two look exactly as my students do when they're not wearing their Sunny Dew orange. How easily we're duped into feeling small. And then I notice the tattoo peeking from beneath the open buttons of the Hawaiian shirt: *I am the master of my fate; I am the captain of my soul.* I am calmed.

I think about Richie and about the classroom full of boys and our discussion about *Invictus* and Nelson Mandela. I am thinking about getting up out of my seat and going over to talk to the kid on the Number 7 train about the lines of the poem now impressed upon his chest, when the train stops and he gets off. An opportunity missed.

Invictus, undefeated. It should be a feeling that everyone has about his life and his job. Most of the COs don't feel that way. Poor image, poor pay, inmate violence, the competition between officers for overtime or different shifts and the stress that results from it—all the things that can defeat you. In fact, it can kill you. The average life span for a correction officer as last reported by the National Institute of Health in 2008 was fifty-nine years. And if the stress doesn't kill you, it leads to high rates of early retirements, impaired health and impaired family relationships, as well as an extremely high burnout rate. For a CO, it's difficult to remain undefeated.

"It's funny how sometimes the people you'd take a bullet for are the ones behind the trigger."
—Ritu Ghatourey

Chapter 25

Freddy

The weekend is upon us, and there's the usual Friday feeding frenzy.

"Mrs. Z, ya think you're going to bring the cart by here?" It's not a yell. Freddy has put forth the question much too politely for it to be confused with a demand. Intentionally so. Freddy knows how to get what he wants.

I'm rushing past classroom 1, but double back—"Before you go, I'll be back."

And I'm true to my word. With a couple of minutes to spare, I push the cart into the room and my two most avid readers, Freddy and Jax, are up in a flash.

They're both examining the cart's contents from A to Z—our alphabetized collection of sorts. Freddy pulls one book off the shelf, reads the back jacket and puts it back in its place. He pulls another one out.

"Oh, I read that already." It goes back on the shelf.

Jax offers his recommendations. He points to a small Perma-bound novel, *Revolver*.

"This is a good one."

Freddy reaches for it and looks it over.

I'm standing at the end of the cart and watching the two of them. If they had coffee, I'd think I was at Barnes & Noble. Freddy interrupts the thought.

"You know, Mrs. Z, they should have some books about gangs."

I look at him incredulously. I'd rather Freddy ask for books on baseball players, but he wasn't really given many options in his life. I know Little League wasn't one of them.

"Yeah, I mean, books about gangs the way they really are today. Maybe written by gang members."

I want to take Freddy by the hand and walk him to the local public library. I want him to write in the word, gangs, in the online catalog and see the electronic screen buzz and flash and scroll the thousands of titles of books about gangs, by gangs, and against gangs. I want him to see the call numbers, to see the authors, to see the copyright dates. I want him to see how long these gangs have been around. How long these gangs have been the same. How long they have captured young men like him. How long they have held boys like him from becoming men.

"Trust me, Freddy, there are books on gangs. If you want to get rich by being a writer, don't write about gangs." There's a tinge of sarcasm, but his absolute naïveté overpowers me.

I don't even know who's in a gang and who isn't here. There are too many gang members to ask. And whether they're in a gang or not isn't important to me as a counselor or unofficial librarian. It is for our classroom teachers, though. We're pretty careful about who we're putting in a classroom with whom. There's no reason to mix a Crip with a Blood.

We had an administrator come and visit once who was touting cooperative learning, a technique I'd used widely in my ESL days. You group students together—the strongest, the medium and the weakest—into cooperative learning groups. Together, if lessons are designed well, the students can help each other learn and complete learning tasks, cooperatively. Here, cooperative has an entirely different meaning.

In 2011 the FBI identified 1.4 million active street, prison, and OMG (Outlaw Motorcycle) gang members comprising more than 33,000 gangs in the United States. The FBI categorized prison gangs as gangs which begin in jail, not the streets, and operate within the jails and prisons in the United States. They separate them from just regular street gangs, who, through mass media, have become household names like the Bloods or the Crips or through heinous crimes like MS-13 (*Mara Salatrucha*), part of the *Sureno* gang, MS-13, 18th Street, and *Florencia* 13, all the most rapidly growing gangs in the United States. Prison gangs, on the other hand, are the gangs, as a civilian, that I have never or rarely heard of: the Aryan Brotherhood, *Nuestra Familia*, or *La Eme*.

This morning, I walked into room 3 and found Diquan, back from Ad Seg, sitting next to Freddy. An odd combination except when you're trying to survive.

Freddy's in for murder—shooting two gang members for who knows what reason. But even at seventeen, that makes him pretty powerful. And sweet Diquan, C Felony-Robbery, who already lost his brother to the street—for all I know, by Freddy.

A murderer and a thief. An MS-13 and a Crip or a Blood. Whatever the combination. It is not a blending of the good and the good. It is not the strong leading the not strong. It is the weak preying on the weaker.

It is a pattern they both learned early on in the streets. Most juvenile gangs and violence have been attributed to more and more older members being incarcerated and the heavy recruitment of juveniles in schools.

I don't have to read an FBI report to know about it. But in both the murderer and in the thief, I see another story, too.

I called Freddy's mother this week and told him I had made the call. She came and visited him. He called me aside the next day. "My mom came to see me yesterday. Thanks for making the call."

"You're welcome, Freddy."

Freddy's been with us a lot of times before. So far, it's been the gang that wins. This time, the story might be different.

"I love you without knowing how, or when, or from where. I love you simply, without problems or pride: I love you in this way because I do not know any other way of loving but this, in which there is no I or you, so intimate that your hand upon my chest is my hand, so intimate that when I fall asleep your eyes close."
—Pablo Neruda, *100 Love Sonnets*

Chapter 26

Kris and Elliot

Whenever I mention my depleted library and an appeal for donations, I cringe when I see paperback dime store romance novels. They are immediately packed, boxed and sent to Building B—female inmates eat them up.

But I can't say these guys are devoid of romance. They represent an eclectic mishmash of tastes and ideas.

The guys in classroom one have been neglected lately, I'll admit it. And they clamor for the book cart as I walk past this afternoon.

When I poke my head in the doorway, it isn't an appeal for just the cart. It is rather specific.

"Do you have a copy of *The Four Agreements*?"

"Are there any real mystery James Patterson's left—not the new MAX series?"

I'm feeling some level of guilt over not bringing the cart in for at least two weeks.

"I'll check the cabinet, and I promise I'll be right back." And I will. The one thing I try to do here is be true to my word. Not much else rings true.

Before I can turn and be out the door, José shouts back, "Do you have any poetry books?"

Romance, or some odd sense of it.

Sex—yes, they have a very good handle on it.

José is trying to estimate the date that he last attended high school.

"Now, my daughter will be two, and I was home from Lincoln Hall on a Christmas home pass, and she was born in 2010." He smiles. "I was in tenth grade in 2009, miss."

I smile. "I figured you'd have to be home some time during that year, José, if your daughter was born nine months later!"

He laughs.

José is not alone. There are a lot of fathers here. When I interview what I would consider very young boys, I am amazed how often they tell me that their girlfriends are expecting, and they already have another child living with some other girl. It is not uncommon amongst the jail population. At last count, in 2007, the number of parents held in either state or federal prisons had increased by 79 percent in sixteen years. Like José, that accounted for 889,800 men who had fathered 1,559,200 children. Of those, almost 45 percent were under the age of twenty-four—just like José. Of those children, 25 percent were under the age of four and more than 50 percent were under the age of nine. Almost 3 percent of our children have a parent who is incarcerated. José's new baby needs José home for emotional support and for financial support. All those other children need their fathers home, too. That's not possible for all those fathers, but for some of them, like José, whose charges have been nonviolent and recurrent misdemeanors since his early adolescence, better alternatives might have been sought than sending him to jail or a juvenile detention center. His baby daughter thinks so.

And it is obvious that José needs to find other ways to secure his manhood other than fathering a child. Right now, he sees great empowerment in that. That's the only way he knows to seek empowerment. He hasn't learned much else being locked up. He doesn't know anything else.

But the boys know about sex.

There are enough documentaries and movies and papers written about sex and jails and prisoners or the lack of it.

Romance is more nuanced. You'd think there could be none. But why would the human heart abandon its finer features amidst the sharpest edges of its existence? There, it has even more reason to exist.

The boys arrive more sporadically for night school than during the day. They're older, not locked down and practically everyone on the dorm has tried to find a place to go—AA, religious service, Bible study, night school. The inmates dangle onto whatever few programs the budget cuts have allowed to remain.

One by one, my students pick up the Sudoku I've printed or the newspaper to read. Mostly, they chat. Kris is in the back. His lanky frame hangs out of the desk like a pair of pants shrunk too small.

He looks up when Elliot saunters in. "Hey, did she call? The bitch wrote me that she was coming to visit, and she didn't show up," he shouts at Kris.

Elliot walks to the back of the room and slides in next to him.

Kris and Elliot start talking about Taisha, Elliot's girlfriend who is now Kris's.

I don't intend to eavesdrop. It's pretty hard not to. The classrooms are small. There's barely room for nine of us. No one actually gets to hide in the back.

"How can she be your girlfriend, Kris?" I ask innocently. "Where did you meet?"

"Ms. Z. I am the man. All she need to do is see me." Kris gives me a broad, handsome and winsome smile. Probably one that won Taisha over in the first place. Kris and Elliot start to laugh.

Kris explains to me that Taisha came to visit Elliot and eyed Kris in the visitor's room. She stopped visiting Elliot.

Jailhouse romance.

She's been writing him ever since. Kris has her picture over his cot. She comes to visit once a week.

Kris and I know that they've never kissed. Never touched. Never held hands. Never done anything that I'd say looked like romance. Or he'd say came even close to sex. And it all blurs.

Jailhouse romance.

Not sex. So it must be romance.

She writes him. He writes her. They exchange intimate thoughts. Intimate feelings. They have nothing else to exchange.

"What's she going to do when you go upstate?"

Kris smiles assuredly. "Wait." He says it with confidence. It's something he has to believe. Or he wouldn't be able to survive his own long days of waiting.

I know exactly what José wants to do. Why he needs that poetry book. A locked away Cyrano de Bergerac writing some girl faraway—using words so foreign from his own, words he thinks more powerful, more penetrating, more potent. More romantic.

That's all he has.

Jailhouse romance.

Passion still exists outside these walls, because it still flames inside you.

"Hell hath no fury like a woman scorned."
—William Congers

Chapter 27

Dante

Library classifications are a lot more than a bunch of letters and numbers written on a book spine. PR 3361 M 395 2006 isn't just literature—it's British literature, seventeenth and eighteenth century. Actually, a collection of writings by William Congers—"Hell hath no fury like a woman scorned."

And NCC # 14000764 isn't just an inmate—he's young, he's black, and he's got a problem: too many women to handle.

Dante calls out to me as I walk pass his classroom: "Hey, Mrs. Z, can I see you a minute?"

We walk across the hallway and he sits down across from me. Dante is a likeable kid. Always a smile. Congenial. Complimentary. Makes a point of telling me how nice I look. Smooth.

"I need you to get in touch with my girlfriend. It's an emergency."

"What kind of emergency, Dante? You know I don't usually call girlfriends."

Early on, I explicitly detail my phone policy—once

in a while, to a parent or maybe a message to a lawyer. I'm not getting involved in delivering any cryptic messages or violating orders of protection.

"No, no, Mrs. Z, she won't take my calls. She stopped talking to me."

"Well, I wouldn't call that an emergency. Maybe an emotional crisis, not an emergency," acknowledging that it must be pretty upsetting but not life-threatening.

"Yeah, I didn't mean to piss her off, Mrs. Z. You're a female, tell me what I should do." And his story began.

I have to laugh when the boys concede—"You're a female, Mrs. Z," or "Mrs. Z, you're a girl," or maybe "You were once a girl"—that's a good one. I'm not sure it's very complimentary.

But I sit and listen as the only female representative they have in their lives right now. They can't be picky.

His old girlfriend had "something" of his that she was holding. But Dante wanted that "something" back, so he HAD to get in touch with her. Problem was it would make his new girlfriend mad.

So he was totally up front with her. Honesty—an attractive trait in a man.

His new girlfriend was okay with it. She understood that he had to get that something back. So he reached out. He asked his old girlfriend for the something back.

"And Mrs. Z, she told me she don't have it anymore." He fumed. "And that's bullshit, 'cause she had just told me a week ago that she had it."

The something was missing—that mysterious who knows what was gone, and Dante wanted it back.

"Do you really believe that she didn't have it, Mrs. Z?"

It really didn't matter what I thought. Dante could have asked me that a week ago. He hadn't.

Instead, he did what his instincts told him he should do.

Now, I should mention what Dante's charges were: criminal sales and criminal possession. Of a controlled substance. So the more he talked about the "something," I couldn't help but think it only could be one thing. But neither of us said it. Right now, he wasn't talking to me about drug sales. He was talking to me about his problems with women!

And his solution to the problem: "And so I wrote my old girlfriend a letter."

Cyrano de Bergerac wrote letters. Albert Einstein did not.

"What kind of letter did you write, Dante?" My question probably pretty similar to his present girlfriend's— well, probably a lot tamer one.

And herein the rest of his tale:

"Well, Mrs. Z., I kind of told my old girlfriend that I still had feelings for her. That I wanted things to be different. That I wanted things to go back to the way they had been." *Smooth.*

"You lied?" He wouldn't be the first guy to do so, and he didn't have to be in jail.

"Well, I had to get that thing back."

"What she do? Tell your present girlfriend?" I was certain that I was right.

He shook his head. "Worse, Mrs. Z. She went and took a picture of the letter and posted it on Facebook."

I knew then and there that I was old. Modern technology had exceeded my imagination.

Dante leaned forward, almost begging me, beseeching me for an answer. "I don't know what to do, Mrs. Z. My new girlfriend won't talk to me. And my old one still won't give me back my stuff."

"You ever hear the expression, 'Hell hath no fury as a woman scorned,' Dante?"

He shook his head.

"Do you know what that means?"

He looked as confused.

"Well, it means that even if you're in hell, it's not as bad as if you really make a woman angry."

And I added, "You have two women really pissed at you."

"You're not kidding. Whadda ya think I should do, Mrs. Z?"

"Nothing."

Now, he looked at me with an even more confused expression.

"If you want my opinion, do nothing. Give it some distance. Let them calm down. Sometimes, it helps to let people's anger rest."

He pondered the option. "I think maybe you're right, Mrs. Z. I can't see them for a while anyhow."

And after a half hour of talking about female" problems with Dante, I saw a little door open amidst our conversation.

"You know, Dante, the way I see it—maybe this was a blessing in disguise. I think God was really taking care of you. I think this wasn't about those girls at all. I think maybe it was about not getting that "something" back 'cause I have a feeling it wouldn't have brought you to a good place."

He sat up straight in his chair, and his eyes opened wide, as if we had both experienced a shared revelation. Like the burning bush. He looked at me with the same wonder that surrounds miracles.

"Mrs. Z, I thought the same thing! I was sitting in my cell last night, and I thought the same thing. That there was a reason for all of this—that God didn't want me to get my stuff back. That this was for my own good."

"I'd have to agree, Dante."

He got up to leave, content that he wouldn't be speaking to either of those two girls. Content that he wouldn't be getting that something back. Content that God was taking care of him, and it was all for his own good.

I got up and was certain that we had both witnessed a miracle.

"Without a Coca-Cola, life is unthinkable."
—Henry Miller

Chapter 28

Graduation—Pizza, a Handshake, and a Bottle of Coke

One of my kids' favorite books when they were little was *Pat the Bunny*. Turns out that it's on the top ten list of children's books for years. With good reason, too.

Its multi-textured pages provide a tactile as well as a reading experience. Add a mother's or father's or auntie's or uncle's warm lap, or a grandma's mushy embrace, or grandpa's strong grasp, and it's sheer delight for any small child—well for that matter, for anybody!

Touch is a delightful human experience.

I just took touch for granted—in a handshake, a friend's warm welcoming embrace, my husband's hurried brush of a kiss. I never considered the warmth of the body sitting next to me on the subway, mostly just the inconvenience or discomfort of their space.

Then, one day, sitting across from one of the newer students, it all came rushing at me.

How untouched these humans' lives were now spent.

I'm one of the few staff members who will shake hands with the students. I don't know if I am breaking any rules. I know I am breaking customs.

When I first started, it just seemed logical to introduce myself, so I shook the student's hand. He looked shocked. I couldn't imagine why.

And then, there was the next one, and the next one, and the next one.

I noted the responses: Some did seem shocked, others hesitant while others seemed to have forgotten that it was a customary way to say hello.

For me, it helped pry open closed doors so much more easily than I might have thought. Just by showing some small measure of respect.

There is no touch here. With good reason. God knows the danger that touch imposes here. But there is no touch here. Nothing.

Human beings separated by shackles. Separated by cells or metal corners of a square table. Human beings separated by shoulder-high dividers in a visitor's room. Fathers who see newborn infants across from them. Deprived of the opportunity to feel their newborn skin. To smell their newness. To breathe the freshness of their skin.

There is no touch. Teachers do not lean over desks hovering close at hand. Teachers do not place an encouraging hand on a discouraged shoulder.

There is no touch. Gloved hands frisk you down. Gloved hands shake down your cell.

And then, I was invited to graduation. I'm told that at some jail schools, they have regular graduation ceremonies. Here, the students are allowed to come into the chapel for our hour-and-a-half ceremony. Whether we wear caps or gowns or throw tasseled mortarboards in the air, the fact that our students get their GED or some go on to earn their high school diploma is quite an accomplishment. Almost 48 percent of local jail inmates haven't finished high school, probably one of the factors that contributes to their being there. And only about 26 percent have the chance to get that GED before they're released. Even for those sent upstate, the chances of completing that GED are pretty difficult. Budget cuts have slashed programs once offered by New York State. Sean Pica, executive director of Hudson Link for Higher Education in Prisons, a nonprofit that helps facilitate educational opportunities for inmates in New York State, suggests that not investing in school programs in our jails and prisons is just not good public policy— without providing educational opportunity, we are simply warehousing people and waiting for them to reoffend and to warehouse them again. I am so thankful that we're not warehousing our sixteen-, seventeen-, eighteen-, nineteen-, and twenty-something-year-olds. I am thankful that they are still entitled to an education under the New York State Education law and I am thankful that we have graduation, with or without the Coca-Cola and pizza.

We do have a speaker—who shakes each student's hand.

Our school principal shakes each student's hand.

Each teacher can shake a student's hand. Mrs. P can even give a hug or two.

And each student can shake each other's hand or give a high five or salute, or choose to congratulate each other in whatever way they see fit.

We order pizza and Coke. Pizza and Coke for guys without Pizza and Coke for a long time. Some, for maybe a year. Others, for maybe two.

And we have a ceremony. We say, "Congratulations!" And we handshake and we hug. And we eat.

And as Pica has himself experienced with other inmates upstate, our boys' successes could be crafted by some TV executive as an after-school special.

Our boys are lucky. Since 1994, jails and prisons have tightened their educational budgets, and Congress banned inmates with felony convictions from getting Pell grants to help pay the tuition for college credits while they were incarcerated. "Lock 'em up and throw away the key." Everyone wanted to get tough on crime, but didn't think about the consequences of the approach. The good news? The rate of incarceration, which had been trending upward from 307,276 prisoners in 1978 to a high of 1,615,487 in 2009, is finally starting to drop—well, a smidgen—1.7 percent (or by 27,770 inmates) to about 1,571,013 prisoners. Can you imagine 1.5 million people locked up? The high school dropout rate has dropped, too—down to 7.4 percent in 2010 from 12 percent in 1990. That's an improvement, too. It would make sense to grab those dropouts who end up in jail (and there's a lot of them) and educate them while they're here. Turns out that their being dropouts is one of the biggest factors in contributing to their arrests.

So our principal reads a boy's name, and he rises from the pew. And he smiles. Those boys smile like I haven't seen them smile for a long time. Some, for maybe a year. Others, for maybe two.

And I bet, if we took away the pizza and Coke, they'd still smile. That just getting their GED and getting those handshakes and hugs and getting together and being human for just that hour and a half would still make them smile.

There's something delightful about human touch.

And there's something very wrong about taking it away.

"By seeking and blundering, we learn."
—Johann Wolfgang von Goethe

Chapter 29

Damion

I wear many hats.

"One of the students in the computer room wants to see the counselor," my colleague announces outside my cubicle as I type in the name of a new student into the computer.

Counselor is my main job description; librarian is one I added as an adjunct, or one I sneaked in.

But when one of the students asks to speak to the counselor, it signals something serious. Generally, they just wait for me to walk past their classroom and holler out my name.

"Hey, Mrs. Z!"

So I got up from my desk right away and left my data entry behind.

When I got to the computer room, I found Damion and signaled for him to come out to speak with me privately, if that's what you'd call the space provided me in an empty classroom at a bare teacher's desk.

He shook his head—to assure me of the lack of urgency—no suicide in mind. Instead, he proclaimed, "All I wanted was the book cart. Where is it?"

I was getting possessive about those books. When I left the cart unattended, too many of them got feet. They were walking right off the cart without leaving a footprint behind—no signed cards left in the box. No evidence of any book thief, just the empty shelves of my cart. So, I decided to lock the cart in my office. Damion had noticed.

"It's in my office, Damion. I'll go get it and bring it in."

A few minutes later, I'm rolling down the hall and I get a few "Hey, Mrs. Z's. There are more than a few Damions looking to sign out a new book. It's Monday afternoon, and it's been a long weekend. The pages between Friday and Monday go much more slowly than during the week.

Damion starts to look through the book selection. He's disappointed.

"Ya, got any hood books?"

Hood books are in great demand. I remember watching a version of *Romeo and Juliet*—with Leonardo DiCaprio. I'm wondering if they'd consider that in the category. I doubt it.

There's a guy in the jail here that wanted to teach Shakespeare. He runs the Drug and Alcohol Program and approached me about it. I'd jump at it in a minute. Maybe we'd convince Damion that *Romeo and Juliet* was a hood book, too. But things like that don't happen here.

I've read about things like that happening, though. Heard a woman speak once at one of our superintendent's conference days who had written a book about her experience teaching Shakespeare somewhere in a Massachusetts jail. I bet they've already tried that in New York City.

But we're little, and the jail I'm in is on a big, big budget, and that guy I talked about is lucky he still has his drug program. He's not going to ask for books about Shakespeare. He doesn't even have enough of a budget to ask for books from AA.

So I'll figure out a way to get Damion his hood books. Maybe look for one that has two gangs, two star-crossed lovers, and ends with everyone realizing that hate and violence destroy lives. Wouldn't that be a novel idea?

Nothing on my cart seems to grab Damion. "You got any self-help books?"

I think to myself, *now this is a new one. Maybe my next order will include Dr. Phil.*

The best I can offer is *The Four Agreements.*

He takes it. Walks away a satisfied customer. I wonder what help it might offer him. The cart is always a wonder. It holds the possibility of creating wonderful things.

"Hate evil, love good; maintain justice in the courts.
Amos 5:15 (NIV)

Chapter 30

Laquan

Laquan shuffled into Mrs. P's room along with the other students. Since he was new, I'd see him in the next few days, but Janet grabbed my arm. She whispered, "I think he's Special Ed. And he's very agitated. You need to see him today."

I trusted her thirty years of special education experience, and as soon as Laquan turned around, I knew, too. I'd assume anybody would know—well, any educator. But we'd become accustomed to not assuming anything.

Laquan certainly wouldn't be the first Special Ed student to pass without notice when processed into the jail. It is generally believed that up to 77.5 percent of school-eligible youth under eighteen who have been incarcerated or have been placed in some kind of a detention center are in need of some kind of special education services. In contrast, typically 9.1 percent of students in public schools require these services.

Laquan was severely cross-eyed and wore a pair of thick black Coke bottle eyeglasses to compensate. Very few children suffer the burden of strabismus nowadays—it's a long ago problem that is now surgically treatable or at least minimized. To be truthful, I hadn't seen someone as cross-eyed as Laquan since I was a kid, long before surgery was an option.

"Hi, Laquan. I'm Mrs. Z, and I meet all the new students." My rehearsed opening lines. His response—nervousness and agitation. Edgy. He began to stammer. Then, stutter. He stuttered so badly that I could hardly make out what he said. To whatever it was, I smiled. From whatever it was, I tried to glean a glimmer of a smile. Laquan wore none.

"Why don't we go down the hall and talk for a few minutes, Laquan?" I asked as calmly as I could. Almost like coaxing a kitten down from a branch too high on a tree. "It will only take a second."

He got up slowly, reluctantly glancing back at Janet for guidance. She nodded approval. And then he followed me.

Laquan didn't smile; he didn't make eye contact. He hung his head deliberately down toward the floor as if he was awaiting my disapproval. All I could see was the top of his shaven head. His head would bob up and down when he answered. Like a buoy amidst the bay, marking time with his each emotion instead of the tide.

"Where did you go to school, Laquan?"

"Fir-ssst, I went to thiiiss high schoool, and then, then I got kick-ed out."

"Why?"

"I got really really m . . m. . mad and g . . g . . ot in a fight."

"And then where'd you go?"

He was difficult to talk to. Short answers made long by the sheer labor of his stuttering. It was exhausting.

Turned out he went to different schools. Different towns. Different students. Different fights. He was always getting really mad. But liked helping out. He was learning to clean and mop up.

"You were learning to work as a custodian?"

"Yesss, to help."

"That's a good job, Laquan."

He shook his head. "But I got f. . f ... fired 'cause I got m ... mad."

I didn't need to ask many more questions. It was clear that I needed more information. In about fifteen minutes, Janet and I had figured out that Laquan was probably very mentally challenged. Probably had anger management issues to boot. Use those words with Laquan and it's not likely he'd have a clue what we'd be talking about. Ask him too many questions too fast, and it's not likely he'd have a clue what you'd be asking. Ask him if he was guilty or innocent, and it's not likely he'd know the difference.

After awhile, you know the answers before you ask the questions. We really shouldn't be able to. The highest proportion of students with disabilities in jail are those with emotional disturbances (ED) or learning disabilities (LD), who make up well over 47.4 percent and 38.6 percent of students in detention centers.

"Do you take any medicine, Laquan?"

He nodded his head and looked up at me.

"Are you taking your medicine now, Laquan,?"

And he shook his head. "My Gr . .gr . . anma . .aa, shh . .eezz going to be m . .m . m . ad. Shh . . ez ain't g . . g

. onn . na let me l . . l. . ive with her no more. Plz . . plz ca
. . ca . . ll her." For the first time, he looked directly at me.
He was very frightened. And upset.

He didn't understand that jail might be where he
could be living from here on in. All he was worried about
was how he had made his "Granma" mad. He had no other
concerns—when he should.

When he had walked into Janet's class, he wasn't
labeled anything. No one had designated him as PC, a
person in need of protective custody. A person at risk of
being harmed. He was living amongst criminal minds who
preyed upon the weakest among them. He was just another
victim waiting to happen.

No one noticed his being different. No one dared
notice at his arrest. No one dared when he stood before the
judge. No one dared when he had a lawyer by his side. No
one would have dared to notice if he hadn't come to school.
And even with our noticing, there wasn't much we could
do.

Laquan was pretty much on his own. Laquan was on
his own even when he had never been before. Even when he
never was supposed to be.

I got the details of his IEP—his school report with
details of his deficiencies. His IQ, well below 70. His father,
deceased. His mother, nowhere to be seen. His medication,
required. His reading, about first grade. His emotional
status, disturbed.

I was certain Laquan couldn't understand the charges
or the court or the pleas. His charges—attempted burglary
with a weapon. A broom smashed through a car window. A
friend's. Who he was very mad at. Laquan's been learning

how to help—how to clean and mop. But sometimes, he gets very mad.

The National Collaborative on Workforce and Disability found that juveniles with ED problems had more difficulty communicating with their lawyers, so were more likely to plead guilty, less likely to discuss options, and unlikely to be good candidates for probation, which they often opted for as a means of shortening their jail time but more than often violated—which put them right back in jail. Juveniles with ED problems frequently were serving longer sentences than their "sharper" contemporaries who didn't suffer from those same problems. Laquan was at higher risk and more vulnerable than others.

His lawyer mustn't have understood that. He never asked him about his schooling or his medication. I don't think they spoke much, because I doubt he could have ignored his stuttering. Must have been in too much of a rush—he never left his card, and Laquan can't even remember his name.

Too bad. Laquan's grandmother doesn't know either.

Turns out, though, she's not Laquan's grandmother at all. Just a nice old woman who took him in when he didn't have anywhere else to go, and she didn't have to.

And she'll take him in again "'Cause the child has nowhere else to go. I don't shut the door on any of God's children."

She can't go to court for him though—she's in a wheelchair. Stays home most of the time.

But she told me that Laquan's angry from a long, long time ago. "His Momma and Gramma treated him like no human bein' should ever be treated."

I wondered if they didn't notice his disability either. That no one explained it to them or that they hoped it'd go away.

Sort of like the jail was now.

Sort of like the court system was, too.

I emailed Legal Aid's Social Work Department anyhow.

Several days later, Laquan asked to speak to me. "A la . . la . . dee come and said sh . . sh . . ez going to help . .p me. Her name ez . . ez Li. . li . . na."

"Good, Laquan. I wondered when his lawyer would show up."

"Sh . . sh ee says I ca . . can go ho … home."

Oh, how I wished he were. Without having to plead out to something he obviously couldn't be accountable for. I'd seen it all too many times before. Before jail, a mentally disabled minor. After jail, a mentally disabled felon.

I hoped he had found a friend who'd take a chance of not doing something exactly by the book and doing something exceptional for an "exceptional" individual—even if no one in his life had recognized it up until now.

"Sometimes the heart sees what is invisible to the eye."
—H. Jackson Brown, Jr., *Life's Little Instruction Book*

Chapter 31

Ishmel's Transparency

Almost everything in jail is glass. Almost everything transparent. But not everything seen.

When those doors slam, nothing seems unseen. Every movement, every action, every impulse, probably even every thought is monitored.

Through *Plexiglas*. Or closed circuit TVs. Or watchful eye.

I'm standing at the elevator, waiting to leave for lunch as Ishmel climbs the stairs from the visitors room across from me. There's only a glass wall separating us. As he ascends to the landing, he sees me and smiles. I nod. He turns to make his way past me and flutters me a wave, the kind of bashful little wave that elementary kids do when they meet you in a store or some place outside of school.

The kind of hesitant "Oh, my God, it's my teacher" kind of wave that a sixth grader might make and then protest about to his friends. "You know I hafta say hello. She's my teacher." Roll your eyes kind of wave. And I wave back. I smile.

I don't think anyone's seen him. And I don't think he realizes that he should care whether anyone does or not.

I feel so motherly—as if he were a little boy. Want to run on his side of the glass and tell him, "You do not flutter here. You do not act weak. You do not show how little you really are."

But I don't. I just smile.

I've seen many a "little boy" lurking in this odd assortment of misfits, muggers, and murderers. I look around the jail and see many a little boy in the adults. Their comfort in forming lines. In abiding rules.

Harry Potter was my first clue. The series had hit the school jail's bestseller list. In classroom after classroom, the boys begged for *Harry Potter and the Philosopher's Stone* or *Harry Potter and the Sorcerer's Stone.* Big and small, gang member or "Great Neck nerd," our supply couldn't keep up with the demand.

Those little boys loved the escape. They loved the Hogwarts School of Witchcraft and Wizardry. They despised Lord Voldemort. And cheered Harry's romance with shy and bashful Ginny.

Those car-chasing, action-packed, video game junkies absolutely ravished our collection of Harry Potter, every single volume.

It baffled me. But doesn't anymore.

And like little children needing supervision, everything they do is always being watched. After a while, I think they forget about it. Or after a while, they just don't care.

On my way in and out, I get caught between two electric gates—one closes. Then, the other opens. Like my childhood memory of playing London Bridges. My friends' arms closed round me in song, "take the key—lock her up—lock her up—early in the morning." Swinging back and forth. Then, delight. Now, impatience. Only an inconvenience. Not a sentence. Not uncomfortable at all.

But glassed in all the same. I look through the glass windows of the guard booth and watch the closed circuit TV, at what I think they call the outside parameter, at the lengths of very lonely and empty hallways, except, perhaps, a lone inmate out on a visitor's pass—like Ishmel.

Further down the glass, lots of TVs. A close up of a face. Not an inmate's. A mother and child. The camera panning her reaching down in her purse. The back of some inmates' heads. A flash of orange walking into the room. A span of monitors flash and flicker like an editing room. The actors played by the visitors who've come today. All on the other side of the glass.

Whatever intimate moments jail has left has been edited from their lives. Like a voyeur, a camera captures the details, even the sweet good-byes.

The TV camera closes in on one couple. It pauses. I hear a bark. I watch the TV and see the jail's black Lab, the jail's resident drug dog, pounce in and run toward the female visitor and jump at her bag. I already know the outcome just by watching on my side of the glass.

I come back from lunch and wait for the boys to come up for school. Ishmel is the first to bound in to classroom 2.

"How was your visit this morning?"

He hasn't had a visit from any family member in months.

"Oh, it was only my lawyer, Mrs. Z."

"Oh, hope it was some good news."

"Nah, he's telling me that he can't get the DA to plead out to less than three ... I wanna do SHOCK but he said he can't get me that program."

"That's a shame." SHOCK, a sort of boot camp program for young adults, would reduce his time, and the discipline would do him more good than sitting in a prison upstate for three years.

"Well, my lawyer hasn't come to see me in three months, and I got scratched four times, Mrs. Z. I don't think he's doing his job. I think maybe I coulda got SHOCK if I had a different lawyer. Ya know, I don't got violent charges."

I had seen plenty of boys go onto SHOCK who had far worse.

I thought about Ishmel waving through that glass window this morning. He'd probably been trying to get someone's, anybody's, attention his whole life and waving through glass windows to get it.

"Heroes are made by the paths they choose, not the powers they are graced with."
—Brodi Ashton, *Everneath*

Chapter 32

Choices

"My lawyer's got me into *SHOCK*, Mrs. Z. I don't know when I'm going, but they're putting the papers through."

"That's great news, Stevie. I'm so relieved." And I was. Stevie had been looking at up to two, if not three years, for a burglary charge. Thank God, no one had been at home, and he wasn't carrying a weapon, but it was a burglary just the same.

But like a lot of the other boys, he was eighteen and foolish, and he lacks the education or skills to get a job if he wants to turn his life around when he gets out. Right now, he has just finished his GED—life's looking a little better. Age will provide him a little wisdom. Any alternative to long-term incarceration is ultimately far better than throwing an eighteen-year-old into a prison system that will do him more harm than good.

SHOCK had been developed in federal, state, and county jails and as an alternative for youthful offenders, for one, to serve their full sentence. And boys, like Stevie, receive substance abuse treatment, attend an academic program, and participate in a boot camp-like program that demands military-style discipline, unquestioning obedience, and a rigid and highly structured schedule of hard work and drills. It could be described as being in the Marines while wearing a different uniform. It's tough. Tough to participate in, and tough to stay in. But the trade-off is simple: Stevie can cut off as much as six months to a year off of his three-year sentence. Well worth it.

Right now, there aren't a lot of alternatives to incarceration open to the guys here. There are lots of drug programs, but the ones in the jail have been cut because of budget concerns, so while the boys are here, very few of them are receiving treatment—even when they need some. There are drug programs on the outside, but they are generally outpatient and not aligned with an educational program, or there are so few linked with schools that the demand exceeds the supply.

New York City, having one of the largest populations of juvenile offenders and incarcerated youth, leads the way in trying to design alternative programs, and a lot of them work. Organizations like the Osborne Association and The Fortune Society work directly with the schools on Rikers Island. They try to restore some stability in these kids' lives to diminish their likelihood of return. Drug treatment and counseling, life skills, education, job training, and job placement are key elements. In special cases, there's parenting or HIV education and for some, who are really up against it, rent, clothing, medications, transportation, and maybe, most importantly, education costs.

Alternatives to incarceration just make good common sense: it's an alternative to choosing criminal behavior as a way of life, and it gives the system an alternative to spending

$3.6 million on a prison budget with an average cost of $60,076 per inmate annually. In New York City's Rikers Island, the price tag was estimated to be $167,731 to feed, house, and guard each inmate in 2012, according to the report by the New York City Independent Budget Office.

"We read to know that we are not alone."
—William Nicholson

Chapter 33

Nausan

"Is there anything to read besides James Patterson?" For a lot of the boys, all they wanted to read was James Patterson.

So Nausan's question caught me off guard. Usually at the end of my "first conversation" with one of our students, professionally called an intake, but what a student would probably call an interrogation, I'd always query, "And do you have any questions FOR ME?"

After all, I'd just spent a good forty to forty-five minutes asking quite a few—some of them quite personal; the least I could do was offer the student the opportunity to ask me one or two. But usually they never did.

Mine were pretty generic. "Name?" "Date of Birth?" "Name of last high school?" "What was the last grade you attended?" And that answer became generic, too. Somehow, the answer being "ten"—always ten. Ten seemed to be the magic number for most first-time offenders. Grade ten. Most managed to squeak through grade nine. Up until then, they were just passing and keeping under the radar of the local police. Up until then, a parent—more than likely a single mother or a

189

guardian—was still struggling to keep them under their thumb. Or they were still showing up sometimes to sing in the church choir, or some good-hearted volunteer basketball coach was giving them pep talks about staying on the straight and narrow. But who knows what else was going on inside those adolescent brains? Because by grade ten, classes were being missed and cops were being called and drug sales were going down and gang members were being jumped. Or they were being mistaken for someone else—the "someone else" who had run down the block at the exact same time they were and at the exact same time as the 7-Eleven on the corner was being hit. And it all happened in grade ten.

By tenth grade, most of our students were drowning in the flow of what is now called the school-to-prison pipeline, a description of joint actions taken by school districts, local police departments and courts when students commit minor criminal offenses at school and are subsequently arrested and prosecuted. Kids taken from school to a police station rarely ask for a lawyer, especially if they can't afford one, and despite spending a lot of time in the front of a TV, don't pay attention to Miranda rights, or whether they have waived them.

While waiting for someone to come pick them up, there are an awful lot of kids who make admissions to formal charges without even knowing it. I meet a lot of kids whose lawyers are trying to plea bargain down their already signed guilty pleas. It's not all that uncommon, even if it's not been a recent episode of *Law and Order*.

In October 2012 the Civil Rights Division of the US Department of Justice filed a class action lawsuit against a school district in Meridian, Mississippi, its police department, and the Lauderdale County Youth Court— for advancing a school-to-prison pipeline and punishing students from the Meridian schools through the courts without due process. Pretty serious charges, particularly against public agencies who you might think would have been advocating for children.

In 2011 Chicago's Cook County Board president, Toni Preckwinkle, summarized the real dilemma of the school-to-jail pipeline—resources—ruining children's lives and wrecking taxpayers' dollars. She estimated that the budget for keeping a juvenile in a Chicago jail or juvenile detention center was more than one year's tuition, room and board at Harvard—at the time, about $600 per child, per day.

So Nausan's question caught me off guard. *Anything besides James Patterson?*

I really wasn't familiar with the book inventory in the classrooms. That was the teachers' domain, not my area of expertise. I was the counselor and guidance person, not the librarian. James Patterson? I was certainly familiar with the hundreds of mystery books he had written, not to mention the ones made into movies. Real page turners. The movies with Morgan Freeman were my favorites.

Nausan explained. "Yeah, I've read all of his books already. And mostly, all the other mystery books in the classroom. I was wondering if you had anything else to read."

"Well, honestly, I don't know, but I'll try and get you something else. What are you interested in reading?"

The moment of reckoning. The moment I unknowingly expanded my job description. And with it, our book collection.

"… but I'll try and get you something else to read."

That moment of recognition. That flash of awareness this was a teachable moment. Not quite knowing what the lesson was. And not quite knowing who the student was. For my years of experience had taught me that often it was the teacher who was the student about to receive the lesson. Not the student at all.

Nausan is surprised I've asked him for his input. He seems dumbfounded at first. He's spent years in school without being given choices, and spent years outside of school making the wrong ones.

He hesitates before making a choice, but then answers, "Books on chess and anything to do with real events— history and news and stuff like that. I like real events."

"Nonfiction?"

"Yeah, nonfiction." Now, I'm surprised. The last thing I expected him to ask for was a history book.

"I'll see what I can do about it." I extend my hand to shake his. "Pleasure meeting you. I'll see what I can do about getting you some of those books to read."

He smiles. "Thanks, Mrs. Z."

I smile. Not only because he's such a likeable young man, but because he's had such a powerful influence on me. He's reminded me of the power of books, almost any book—James Patterson, the Bible, a comic, *The 100 Best Jokes*. About the power a book can have when it's the only companion you have in a locked-down cell where you are sitting almost twenty-four hours a day. When you're sixteen or seventeen, or eighteen years old, and you're supposed to be outside and running around on the basketball court, or playing video games, or hanging out with friends, and instead you are lying on a cot by yourself and figuring out how to spend the next fourteen hours that you're awake. That's when a book becomes very powerful.

It has the power to entertain. To enlighten. To refresh the soul. To help you laugh. To comfort. To help you relax. To assuage your anger. To provide you solace. Then a book has the power to provide you the dreamed opportunity of escape.

Nausan walks back to his classroom, and I walk back to my office, now with one more additional job to do—I need to find books about chess and historical nonfiction. The question is, *Where and how?*

* * * * *

There is a power to books. There is a power to reading. There is a power to information.

It's called knowledge. Wisdom grows out of knowledge, and change out of wisdom. There is good reason why a library is important to those incarcerated in prison (and for those not).

In fact, libraries in correctional facilities do many things, and they are testament to how empowerment can not only help inmates, but correction officers, the families of the incarcerated, and society. The New York Public Library is a model for outreach services to diverse populations not traditionally served by the public library system, notably, incarcerated individuals. They provide writing programs, book discussion groups, an extensive lending library, and even a blog when Internet services are available at a facility. The NYPL has created a family-oriented program, Daddy

& Me, a chance for family reconnection and support, where detained parents attend early literacy workshops and record a CD of themselves reading their favorite book to their children.

One of my greatest resources when I first began my job is METRO Special Interest Prison Librarians' Group, hosted by the Metropolitan Library Council in New York City. I discover organizations and networks that support reentry that I didn't even know existed. I network with librarians from other correctional facilities. I exchange ideas. I'm gaining in knowledge, and I'm feeling empowered. I'm becoming more capable at my job because I'm seeking the information I need.

I would be curious to see what would happen if we used a "jail-to-library" pipeline instead of fostering the "school-to-jail" one. What if the courts could see the usefulness of giving these boys information about the consequences of a felony, of providing them information about accessing educational or vocational services and where to get them, of referring them to an information specialist who could answer their questions and offer them what they really need: "Do you need help?" Those are the tools of a good reference librarian. Figuring out what information a person really needs. The courts could do the same thing. Appoint a person. "If you need any help, please contact me.

These boys obviously lack wisdom, but they also lack information.

Tyrone asks me about getting him the paperwork for a Certificate of Relief.

"Mrs. Z, my mother can get me a job in a nursing home when I get out, but I can't have no felony on my record. Can you get me that paper? What do they call it? You know, a conduct order?"

"Do you mean a Certificate of Relief or a Certificate of Good Conduct, Tyrone?"

"Yeah, yeah, that's what I mean. The CO on my tier told me that it will get rid of my felony."

Both Tyrone and the CO lack information. Certificates of Relief, or Certificates of Good Conduct, for that matter, don't "expunge" your felony—nothing erased it. There's no such thing as expunging a felony in New York State. If you pick up a felony at twenty, it stays with you for the rest of your life.

The application that Tyrone's going to be asked to fill out is more than likely to have that one lethal question for any of our boys, "Have you ever been arrested or convicted of a felony? If yes, please explain in the lines provided." It's the kiss of death. Technically, it's discriminatory and a violation of the Civil Rights Act, but it is commonly used by the private sector and goes unchallenged. Well, until an organization, Ban the Box, advocated with the Equal Employment Opportunity Commission for clarification, and yes, the EEOC agreed that an employer would have to have good reason to ask the question before the candidate was even being considered for the job. But everybody does.

Tyrone's lucky in one respect: He has a family member out there looking for a job for him. Securing a job is one key aspect to an inmate's not reoffending. But if you're going to be eliminated as you complete the job application, there's not much of a chance that you're going to find a job.

Tyrone can eventually file for a Certificate of Relief—in three years—because he has only two felonies with the same charges, C felony robbery. But it doesn't expunge his record. The Certificate of Relief will remove anything that might bar him from getting a license—for instance, a hairdresser, but not a health aide, which requires a background check. His conviction will still surface to the top. All the Certificate of Relief says is that he's a good law-abiding citizen since his release. It's up to another compassionate law-abiding citizen to give him a second chance.

Tyrone needs to know this information. He should have known it before he committed his second offense. Maybe if he knew that his first offense, a YO (youthful offender), was sealed but his second was not, he wouldn't have been so quick to reoffend.

These boys need information. They need empowerment. They need knowledge. In here and when they get out. Especially when they get out. Then they really lack the guidance they need. Of course, there isn't a lot out there for them. Support agencies are drying up as quickly as state and federal budgets.

If they weren't locked up in the first place, there wouldn't be reentry. It's an odd term to apply to these boys' return home. Reentry. It smacks of astronauts and moonwalks for me. I am old enough to imagine a space capsule plummeting back to earth and plunging into the ocean, exactly what their reentry is not. But, maybe it is an appropriate image. Reentry. The plummeting back, the plunging forward—a dramatic transition—when we've locked these boys away for months and years on end, and then release them back into the same places, with the same people, and with the same things.

NYPL publishes *Connections*, an annual guide and directory of resources in New York City available to help former inmates when they are leaving correctional facilities. Turn the pages and you find an organization here and one there reaching out a hand to the formerly incarcerated, but there are only a few. It's not nearly enough to reach out to the nearly 25,000 prisoners released every year, and it's probably why nearly two-thirds of them are rearrested within three years. It's probably why Tyrone came back after his first arrest. His mother is certainly trying to keep him out of jail, but just getting him the job in the nursing home isn't the only support that Tyrone needs.

"Tyrone, do you know where 50 Clinton Street is?" I ask. I'm sending him to the New York State Department of Labor office. I know that they have a new program, New York Builds, where private companies are paid to hire formerly incarcerated youth.

"I've already gone there, Mrs. Z. They told me they'd get me a job, but they never came through."

I know that for every "they never came through," there's a boy who "never showed up." That's the reality of the reentry plummet and plunge.

"We meet no ordinary people in our lives."
—C. S. Lewis

Chapter 34

Aidan

Nobody takes the library cart too seriously.

Everyone sees the signing in and out as an exercise in futility. No one really believes that these guys are responsible enough to return the books, that they care enough about anything, let alone someone's or some library's book, to bring it back. They're really surprised when they do.

If truth be told, the books are signed out on a wing and a prayer. Not so much that they be returned. A prayer that reading it might offer some redemptive quality. A crazy thought on my part. A kind of librarian's quixotic quest.

But oh, how these guys tug at my heart, despite the piles of unreturned index cards I assemble in the back of the black plastic catalog that sits atop the top shelf of the cart. They sign their names so carefully upon the author's card. *Kris White ... Maurice Lawrence ... Delan Campbell.* Their names stick with me as much as they stay upon the cards. And then they are gone. And so are the books they signed out. And how or if they touched something is as well. I am left to wonder. It is every librarian's regret.

So I'm straightening the book cart and assessing our

loss of inventory. It's early Monday morning, well before any of the students are being called. Angelo comes down the hall shouting, "Where's the library lady? Hey, library lady!"

I've rolled the cart out into the middle of the coffee room, if that's what you want to call the narrow hallway of a room equipped with microwave, sink, and coffeemaker. And Angelo makes his entrance in with another CO, carrying a huge clear plastic bag—a huge plastic bag filled with books.

One glance through that plastic sends adrenaline through my veins—I see *Ten Mile River, In My Father's House, A Lesson Before Dying*. I see books that I haven't seen in a long time.

The CO puts the bag down and the coffee room goes wild. The verb, cast lots, always held a powerful imagery for me. Now, I understand its connotation.

Sue dives into the plastic bag as I stand by feeling both helpless and bureaucratic. I want to shove her out of the way and scream, "Wait, these books have to be checked in!" until I realize that our check-in is as much a piece of fiction as most of these novels.

Janet is taking a few back to her classroom as I lay a few books on the desk in front of me to clean off with Lysol. Until she reminds me where they're going back to anyway—back to the boys' cells. Anesthetizing them is really pointless.

I have to be fast—the books are going out of the coffee room faster than I can clean them. I grab up as many as I can. The sorting and figuring out which ones come from where can wait until later. This is about survival and getting what you need. Jail is no place for organization or the Dewey Decimal system!

Even for us, things look different in here than they do out there. The way you do things, the things that are important, the things that matter, they all change from the inside out. For us, for a short time each day. For the boys ...

I'm walking down the hall with my file folders in hand past the glass-windowed, carefully watched classrooms, and a familiar voice shouts out, "Hey, Mrs. Z, ya gonna bring in the book cart?"

I go back to get the cart and roll it in before I go to meet our newest student and appreciate the word, clamor as I never do before. The boys rush the cart as kids might an ice cream truck.

It's one of the ways jail changes you.

I walk to classroom 4 and meet Aidan. He's already changed, and I can't possibly know that—I'm just meeting him for the first time, but he's been in jail for a couple of months now. He's been here long enough for some of those changes to begin. Outside, he'd written school off a long time ago. In that magical tenth grade dropout year. Now, he's decided to drop back in.

"No sense in going back to your high school at this point," I say, looking up at him and doing a quick assessment of the situation. "Better to try and get your GED here—make some good out of a bad situation right now."

He nods and gazes at me with the most amazing set of emerald green eyes. They're captivating. Aidan is a beautiful contrast—the full spectrum of humankind. His jail profile listed him as "B" for black, interestingly, a politically incorrect and also imprecise term. But Aidan proved more than just a racial blend, more than a visible harmony between black and white and beige.

"Do you have any questions?" A standard end of interview. Rarely continued.

But today, Aidan asks, "Can I see the book cart? The guys told me you have books I can take back to my cell."

The Aidan I'm meeting today probably contrasts sharply with the Aidan who dropped out of school three years ago. Then, he was bored out of his mind and thought he had plenty else to do. Now, he is bored out of his mind and has absolutely nothing to do.

Aidan is smarter than a lot of other students. He already knows the remedy for his madness—something to read. For a lot of others, I have to offer them the remedy before they find the cure.

"Do you like to read?"

"Yeah, some things." He pauses as if trying to think of the kind of books he likes to read. Instead, he provides me with a more honest and sincere analysis than any educational expert could give, "When I was in school, I didn't think I did, but since I got in here, I've been reading a lot. And I like it."

Because he likes it, and because he does it, I'll bet that his reading has improved. I can't prove it—I've got only my little cart—but bigger programs than ours, like SHOCK, found reading scores going up as high as four or more grade levels for those inmates enrolled in school.

Things look different in here than they do out there.

And I keep thinking about that one CO this morning—I didn't even catch his name. I don't know what tier he's from or where he got those books, but I keep thinking about him. And then it dawns on me.

Someone, somewhere in that jail had collected those books and put them in a clear plastic bag and acknowledged we were a library. The signing in and signing out. The fraudulent card catalog. The delinquent books. It wasn't just a figment of our imaginations. The kids' or mine. I was lending books, kids were borrowing books, and some of them were bringing them back. And one very mindful CO had collected them. In the bottomless pit of property within the enormous cement block of squared-off cells and towers and tiers of a jail, some CO had found books and brought them back. Here. To our school library. A double-sided, three-shelf-high rolling book cart. And Aidan had asked to sign out one of those books.

"Never forget that justice is what love looks like in public"
—Cornel West

Chapter 35

Maurice

"I'm firing my lawyer, Mrs. Z."

It's an endless refrain.

Well, for unpaid lawyers, that is. And that's roughly 90 percent of the students here. Or else they wouldn't be here. They'd be bailed out. At the last official count, in 2009 by the Bureau of Justice, that was actually 82 percent of those incarcerated in a jail or a prison. They had been represented by publicly funded counsel.

I'm not a statistician. All I know is that most of my students have been given a legal aid or court-appointed lawyer instead.

"I think my lawyer's working for the DA. My lawyer hasn't been up to see me in two months. I haven't heard from my lawyer. I keep leaving messages on the voicemail."

And it goes on and on and on.

Pierce asked to see me this morning. I couldn't imagine why; we had just spoken at the beginning of the week.

"I need to know my next court date, Mrs. Z. I want to fire my lawyer."

Not surprising.

When we had last spoken and he had told me his lawyer's name, I already knew that Pierce was doomed.

I know when a kid is given an overly subscribed legal aid lawyer. I never say so. But by now, I've compiled my own list.

And I know the difference between the court appointed lawyers and the privately retained ones—maybe eight months or three years. Or maybe two or seven. Or seven or nine. Or walking with a felony or with a misdemeanor. The plea bargains are different: Privately retained lawyers get you out of jail time.

Public defender offices are understaffed and underfunded. They rarely have the necessary resources to provide an adequate and effective counsel for the poor, minority and indigent populations they represent. On the fiftieth anniversary of *Gideon v Wainwright* (1963), the Supreme Court case which upheld a defendant's right to counsel provided by the court if they could not afford one, the Brennan Center for Justice concluded that it would make much more sense to help indigent defendants have competent and adequate counsel than to continue to support an ever-expanding system of mass incarceration. In that fifty-year span, mass incarceration has grown from 217,000 to 2.3 million people, of which 60 percent are African American or Hispanic, due in part to their arrests and incarcerations for low-level, nonviolent crimes as a result of what University of North Carolina Law School professor, Gene Nichol termed "tawdry treatment" while proclaiming "lofty pronunciations on equality."

So when my students complain to me about their legal aid lawyers, I give them my standard line. I remain politically correct. It kills me. They should present me a prize: "A free lawyer is not a bad lawyer—just a busy lawyer."

"But, Mrs. Z, it's the third time they called me for court, and I all I got was bullpen therapy."

And it was true. A lot of the time, my students would be carted off to court and put in a holding cell. When they weren't called, they could be assured one thing: two bologna sandwiches and two containers of warm milk—bullpen therapy. And then, they'd be carted back for yet another day at court.

Hey, I'm not saying it's not difficult for the lawyers, too. I am sure they hear "I'm innocent" a million times in a lifetime.

That one in a million probably seems pretty implausible.

Maurice had one of the kindest and gentlest faces in or out of jail. His huge brown eyes had fanned eyelashes that were simply wasted on a boy. I'd kill for them. He had an irresistible smile. It bespoke volumes. He stood tall and straight and confident and wasn't ashamed to use God and blessed in the same sentence, or even say those words aloud.

"Have you ever been arrested before?" One of my standard questions.

"No, ma'am."

"Your first offense?" He nodded. "What are your charges?"

"Having a gun, ma'am. But it wasn't mine. The police made a mistake."

My first instinct—proceed forward. Jump from one perfunctory question to the next. Like skipping on stones to cross a stream. One question. Jump to the next. Check another off my list. Name? Jump. Address? Find out what you needed to know. Find out any other details later. There was little to dispute, with all the boys: The police were always making mistakes.

"What's your address, Maurice?"

"Right now, ma'am?"

I looked up from my pad. "Yes." It seemed a simple enough jump.

"My family doesn't have one, right now. We're staying at the shelter in Bellport. My Mom's waiting for a place to stay."

I stopped moving so fast.

"Where were you going to school?"

"Bellport High School."

"But it says here that you were arrested in Hempstead—that's a pretty long way from Bellport." And it was. It was probably about 40 miles geographically, but it was a pretty long way from the crime and poverty that had come to reside in Hempstead over the last fifty years.

Maurice used to live there. His sister, still.

He had come to see her dressed up for her senior prom. At his grandmother's. In Hempstead. Where he used to live. But not anymore. Now, he lived at his mother's. Well, not quite. He lived with her. In Bellport. But that night, he wasn't. He was in Hempstead.

The boys across the street decided to drive to see the prom. Maurice got in. Way over his head.

"The police pulled us over, ma'am. *Founded* a gun under the seat. The boys said it was mine. They already was arrested before."

And he ended up in the wrong place. He ended up

there at the wrong time. He was with the wrong people. There was nothing right about it, and it was an awful big price to pay.

"But my lawyer says that I can go home." Maurice smiled at me optimistically. "God is good. The charges be dropped."

And Maurice's mom couldn't afford to call. And she couldn't afford the drive.

So Maurice waited for his lawyer instead.

"My lawyer says that he can get a plea."

And soon Maurice's hope began to fade.

"My lawyer says that if I take a 6/5 ..."

Well, he already sat waiting for justice just to take a peek. Four months would make it complete. If he'd only take the plea ...

And Maurice's mother still couldn't afford to call. And she still couldn't afford the drive.

So Maurice waited for his lawyer instead.

"Mrs. Z, I'm going to take the plea."

Maurice's hope disappeared.

And Maurice left.

Not to go home.

And not with his mother. (Not while he's on probation. That's one of the obstacles he'll face with public housing).

But he's out. Innocent, but pled guilty.

Homeless. Uneducated. Unemployed.

Released without a future.

"Necessity never made a good bargain"
—Benjamin Franklin

Chapter 36

Innocent Until Proven Guilty

And so Maurice pled guilty when he had proclaimed his innocence. Dr. Vanessa Edkins, a psychology professor at the Florida Institute of Technology, and Lucian Dervan, assistant professor of law at Southern Illinois School of Law, called this the "prisoner's dilemma." Maurice did have one: What do I have to do to go home?

Turns out that's exactly what the study's participants' rationale was, too. Over half (56.4 percent) of the participants pled guilty when innocent to cheating on a test (when they didn't) just because they simply wanted to go home. Of course, they really weren't locked in, but the simulation was real enough.

I'd like to give Maurice and my other students a book with that short story, *The Lady or the Tiger?* by Frank Stockton, the one that you give seventh graders to read and discuss about facing dilemmas and making choices. Plea bargaining can be likened to the story's spectator trial in the arena with the accused man facing two closed doors, one with an unknown maiden whom he will be forced to marry or the other, a tiger. The accused must choose which one to open. And the accused's only advocate, the princess, whom he loves, must sacrifice her own needs by losing him to the mystery maiden, but will she? Can the accused trust that she has made the best decision for him when she directs her eyes toward the door he should choose? Mightn't she prefer his death to the tiger than suffer living a life knowing he is with another? Which door should he choose? Which plea should he take? Such is the "prisoner's dilemma." *Which is the better choice?* And like the accused man with the beautiful yet, as Stockton describes her, "barbaric" princess, *Can I rely on my lawyer to advocate the best choice for me?*

Ironically, Edkins and Dervan found that the more innocent a defendant, the more likely to confess to a guilty plea in return for an incentive like going home or taking probation.

In 2012, 97 percent of convictions in our courts were the result of plea bargaining. It is unclear how many of those were actually innocent. Based on Edkins and Dervan's results, the study suggests that the number of innocent defendants who would likely confess could be as high as 56.4 percent.

I'm a librarian, not a lawyer. I leave the lawyering to the lawyers. I leave the shelving of books to me, but it's awfully hard as a researcher, to ignore statistics or to avoid article after article in the newspapers about how a plea bargain mightn't be a bargain at all. It may very be well just one more rip-off.

But people are starting to take notice. Last year, Supreme Court Justice John Paul Stevens wrote for the majority in *Padilla v Kentucky* that plea bargaining is a "critical stage" in the legal rights of the defendant as part of his Sixth Amendment rights. The Supreme Court was demanding more effective assistance of defense counsel for defendants like Maurice. The prosecutors concluded that more than half of the offenders had not completed high school—just like Maurice—and in the *Padilla* case, Mr. Padilla could not speak English. The public defenders had an obligation to provide their clients with "thorough and effective counsel."

All of this is very real for me. It is not something that is happening in a building in Washington DC, which ironically bears the motto, Equal Justice Under Law.

Maurice leaves guilty and on probation; Dyshone the same. Stevie has made a better deal—cutting his time down by half. Some never even appear in court. They don't choose their lawyers. It is the luck of the draw. They are court-appointed for them.

The boys complain that they're not getting a fair shake. Truth is that plea bargaining has become so much a part of our legal system that conviction rates for private and public defenders are about the same. However, and it's a big however, being sentenced to incarceration afterward was very different. For defendants found guilty with publicly financed counsel, 88 percent federal, and 77 percent state, were sentenced to jail time, serving a sentence of incarceration, compared to defendants with privately retained lawyers, whose pleas avoided doing time.

There's plenty of reasons why our boys should be reading books. They need to be one step ahead of the legal counsel they've been assigned. That fair shake they talk about hasn't really anything to do with the lawyer they've been assigned. It has more to do with the education they've received and what they're able to do with it.

No matter what system they've participated in, they've been shortchanged. Picking up a book just might be the first time they can change the odds in their favor.

How well they read can determine how well they can advocate for themselves. That's empowerment.

"If you judge people, you have no time to love them."
—Mother Teresa

Chapter 37

Kris Goes Up Top

I found out this week that Kris had been transferred upstate—"up top," as the boys put it. I think if you look at a map of New York, most of the state prisons are all at the top of the map.

I knew that he was getting state-ready for a while, but getting ready to leave and actually being transported to an upstate prison can take a long time. Sometimes, a couple of months. Sometimes, almost half a year.

I didn't even have a chance to say good-bye. I often don't. I've learned not to make attachments to these students as I might when I had taught a "regular" high school. Not likely we're going to touch base via Facebook. Not even when they get out. It'd be too much of a risk.

It's tough to want everything for a human being, and do everything you can for a human being, and then have nothing to do with them after they leave.

Kris was one of the few students I wished I could have said good-bye to. There are just some kids you desperately want to make it, and Kris was one of those kids.

I wished I could have given him some parting words of wisdom. A quote from Henry David Thoreau on success as I did with my ESL students when they left. Or maybe I could give him something affirming from Nelson Mandela or Dr. Martin Luther King. Or a book. Some kind of book.

When I heard Kris had left, I wished I might have been able to have given him some book of worth to take with him on his journey. A gift. Something to value as he made his way upstate into a gift-less world.

I thought about what book I might choose. I remember reading a list once of the Top Fifty Books To Read Before You Die—mostly a course in British Lit—but what sticks in my mind in the middle of this impressive list is *Winnie the Pooh.*

I thought of Kris. And Christopher Robin. And Winnie the Pooh and Tigger. And Piglet. Their simple wisdom. And how simple Kris's life might have once been.

I remembered a conversation with his mother. I called to get his Social Security number and mentioned what a respectful young man he was. (He is.)

She welled up. "Thank you, ma'am, for saying such nice things about my baby. Nobody says too many nice things about him."

"Well, he is very respectful, Mrs. White. His teacher and I both appreciate his good manners. You did a good job raising him to be respectful of older people."

This woman seemed so relieved. She seemed exonerated. I had somehow pardoned her from sharing in Kris's burglaries and school suspensions and previous scrapes with the law. I had somehow patted her on the back and told her, "I know you did the best job you could. I know you tried."

"Thank you, Mrs. Zeman. I appreciate all you said." She knew there would be a long absence before she would see her son. Hundreds of miles, instead of a few, would now stand in their way.

I really liked Kris. I knew most people did.

His mother loved him. She didn't love what he had done. And she had tried her best to make him "do good."

She had tried to have him sit still in church. To go to school. To study for tests. To say "Please" and "Thank you." To do all of the things a mother should. And now we sat on opposite ends of a phone, feeling the same way about her son. Wishing he could "do good."

I didn't know if a book would do the trick. It wouldn't matter if it be *Winnie the Pooh* or *Shakespeare's Works*. Kris wouldn't be taking any books along.

He had to leave every remnant of his life here behind. Everything. Gift or no gift. Books. Photographs—mother or girlfriend. Letters. Everything. When he left, there wasn't even his shadow left upon the sidewalk.

My wish for words of wisdom. His mother's prayers for guidance. These would be left to the unknown. A wiser and older inmate. A compassionate chaplain. Maybe a library over brimming with books.

Our hope that there'd be a voice—some voice— reminding him that he could do good.

Some unknown voice—urging him to do good.

I wished I had been able to say good-bye.

"Just as a candle cannot burn without fire, men cannot live without a spiritual life."
—Buddha

Chapter 38

David's Dreads

Evangelization is commonplace here. Without the evangelists.

A Bible can thump all by itself. Boys locked up in Ad Seg all alone with a Bible find conversion experiences. Then, when they are out, find themselves converting each other.

But it is not only scripture that triumphs here. There is a host of other religious conversions, too.

David left a note for me this morning with whomever had night school last night:

> Call my lawyer and tell him that I need to get 1.5 to 3 years by the end of March and that I need a court order saying that I'm a Rastafarian before I go upstate. I don't want to get a haircut.

These boys can be a demanding lot.

    a. I am not David's legal assistant, and

    b. I certainly am not going to tell his lawyer what to do.

And I don't know anything about court orders and Rastafarians. I think David might have the process a bit confused.

I do know that I've had prior Rastafarian converts—Kris White being one of them. Most of them didn't have a clue that the *Holy Piby* was their scripture or knew who Marcus Garvey, founder of the Black Star Line, was. They had no idea that he proposed a shipping line that would transport African-Americans back to their homeland, Africa, in the 1920s and 1930s. Nor did I, until their "conversions" prompted my research. What did appeal to them though was the Rasta's dreadlocks and their use of cannabis—to them, weed.

Jail demands some modifications to religious practices—no Manischewitz at Passover, no wine at communion, no marijuana at Rastafarian gatherings. But Muslims wear kufis and Jews, yarmulkes. Christians, whether Protestant or Catholic, wear rosary beads around their neck. Crosses and Christ head tattoos abound. And Rastafarians embrace their dreadlocks so tightly that this religious practice is not to be taken from them when transported up top, when everyone else is mandated to shave their head.

On this point, David was correct. If he converted, he'd hang onto the dreadlocks he'd clumsily twisted onto his hair. It was unfortunate, though, that David had some of the worst dreadlocks I had ever seen. Perhaps because he had twisted them himself. Perhaps because he had no beeswax to spin into his hair. But I suspected it was because David was going bald. His dreadlocks, unlike Bob Marley's, were sparse and thinly matted. There were gaping bald patches in between. I don't know if it was a hereditary condition or the result of stress: but David had very little hair—barely enough to comb, let alone to twist. His conversion experience, for all its effort, was going to prove futile within a year or two.

I knew the process, and it wasn't a court order. It was a simple form signed off by one chaplain and approved by another. Simple enough.

I walked around the corner to the group of chaplains' offices. I had hoped to find Larry, my Episcopal minister ex-hippie friend, but instead found one of the Catholic deacons—Deacon John, always congenial but serious. I did not like this being the intermediary between God and David's hair-raising experience.

"Hate to bother you," I interrupted his homily writing. "One of the boys wants to change his religion, and I know there's a way to go about it."

"What religion, and what's his name?" he answered quickly without protest and without concern that he was giving up one of his flock.

"Uh, Rastafarian—the kid's name is David Hunter."

"Oh, he's being transferred upstate?" He, too, seemed to know about the haircut loophole. It didn't seem to bother him. He pulled out a huge computerized daily printout of the inmates and used his finger to navigate the H's. "Here he is." And his finger scrolled sideways from column to column until it stopped at David's current religious preference: *PRO*. "I see he's currently listed as Protestant."

He pulled a form from the drawer and started to fill it out. And chatted.

"You know our jail doesn't recognize Rastafarian as a religion. Right now, he'll be changed to *OTHER*." He kept writing.

I looked over his shoulder at the long list of names and religions next to them: *PRO, CATH, JEW, MUS, NONE,* or *OTHER*. Those were the choices. I mused over *NONE*. I wondered at what point in the arrest process did you ask God's mercy.

Deacon John looked up. "You know, some of these guys want to switch from Catholic or Protestant to Jewish—the food's much better."

I had never thought about it. I just knew that the rabbi did have a rather formidable gathering on Monday nights.

Deacon John continued, "Well, I am more than happy to bring them the form, but I do mention that if they convert that they have to be circumcised."

He didn't laugh; he didn't even smile. I thought it was worth a Jerry Seinfeld guffaw. He added, "Few of them do."

He handed me back the completed form. "Just have him sign it and return it to me. I'll pass it on to the Protestant chaplain. When he goes upstate, they'll list him as Rastafarian—they have many more choices up there."

I considered the options. Considered the benefits. Buddhists, vegetables. Hindus, meditation. None? There was no benefit to having "none" in here. What I noticed most here was that very few had abandoned prayer.

"How are you doing?" A question I often asked. Over and over again, the boys' answers were almost the same.

"I'm just praying every day that I get through this." "I'm relying on God to help me." "With the help of God, I get through each day." And on and on.

The funny thing is that in this awful place, I see God more often every day than I've seen Him anywhere else in my life. Even God wearing dreadlocks.

"The school of hard knocks is an accelerated curriculum."
—Menander of Athens

Chapter 39

Jacquell

The word diminutive is one of those words that you remember. It suggests many things. Small. Tiny. Fragile.

Lilliputian for Gulliver. Cute for cheerleaders. Fatal for an inmate.

Particularly when coupled with naive and guileless.

Jacquell was new—he had never been arrested. He didn't know anyone who'd ever been arrested. No one in his family. Nor any of his friends, well, up until now. Being in jail was something completely new.

When Jacquell and I sat down to talk, I realized how new he really was.

"What are your charges, Jacquell?"

"$2,500."

I was puzzled until I realized he was talking about bail, "charges" to him.

"No, no, Jacquell—why did they arrest you? What did they say you did?"

Now, he looked at me less quizzically.

"Oh, robbery …"

Jacquell didn't look like a mastermind. Or a ringleader. Or like an expert shoplifter or iPhone thief. On a hunch, I asked, "Were you co-ded?" He had to have been arrested with someone else more experienced than he.

"I don't understand what that means."

"Do you have a codefendant? Were you arrested with someone else?"

Jacquell nodded and then added, "I was standing there, while my friend robbed someone else. He grabbed someone's phone and ran. I got arrested, too."

And I nodded.

How often had my mother's admonition been: "Be careful who you hang out with."

Or had I heard the age-old adage, "Birds of a feather stick together."

No sense in repeating that now. Jacquell was already stuck, and I am certain that he had heard it a million times before.

"Where did you go to school, Jacquell?"

"Well, I had been in Hempstead High School, but I only came in ninth grade, and then I moved back to Jamaica for a while after I got in trouble there."

"What school in Jamaica? I live in the city."

He smiled. "No, Mrs. Z …," and now he lilted into a deeper West Indian melody, "I be from the island, not the city."

I laughed.

Jacquell knew very little about being in jail. About going to court. About anything to do with this whole messy process.

He didn't know his lawyer. He didn't know his charges. He didn't know his court date.

But he was learning.

There was no dictionary of terms to give Jacquell. No reference book collecting dust on a shelf that might prove useful to him. Life on life's terms would define the words. Only jail would teach him about jail.

"My father gave me the greatest gift anyone could give
another person;
he believed in me."
—Jim Valvano

Chapter 40

Jacquell's Father

Jacquell asked to see me soon after.

He had been "scratched"—they hadn't called him for court. He wanted me to reach his father and tell him not to come.

He was upset because the other guys on his block were making him "pay rent." They were asking him to give them food for safety and shelter. Different currency. Same economy.

Jacquell was hungry.

"Co-ded."

"Bail."

"Plead out …"

Not just words to be memorized. Words experienced. The kind of words with the greatest meanings of all.

No matter how diminished Jacquell's stature might become, there would no longer be any sense of that word, diminutive, about him. Or any sense of the word, naive.

I did call Jacquell's father to tell him not to go to court. He was already on his way. He thought it best that he at least show up to talk to the judge.

Like father, like son. Or, like son, like father.

I didn't want to disappoint him. But he was as new as Jacquell to this inefficient and overtaxed justice system. "Naive."

"Jacquell wanted to know if you were able to post bail with his brother's car." And as calmly as someone comments while issuing an alarm, I added, "Jacquell is not in the safest environment." Almost as reassuringly as the captain on the Titanic must have snapped, "Step lively onto the lifeboats, please."

How much could I raise his alarm? Particularly a parent uncertain of his child's rescue. Particularly a parent uncertain if he should rescue his child.

Everyone who inhabits this dark and dangerous place, even those who work here, lives in the clouded and confusing blindness of justice, knowing that her blindness offers little protection for the innocent (or barely innocent) in here and wishing her blindfold would fall for a couple of hours of the day.

No one can possibly know how dark or how dangerous this place is until they pass through those gates and live it. No one could possibly define the many words that Jacquell is yet to learn. I only wished he could learn them somewhere else.

Jacquell's "education" here will cost the county quite a sum—roughly $16,000 a month. A lot more than the $12,000 a year it might have cost. A lot more than it would have cost the state or the county or even some philanthropist or two to kick in an extra dollar or two to fund a program or two for at-risk kids like Jacquell and his friend.

But New York State has a lot of Jacquells and New

York City has even more, and Hempstead more, and …

Jacquell's father just called.

There was no one at court to talk to. He didn't find out who Jacquell's lawyer is. Yet. So he doesn't know how to post bail. Even if he could.

He's missed visiting hours today. There's none tomorrow. It's Thanksgiving.

He's learning, too.

My mother used to call all of this the school of hard knocks—one more phrase for Jacquell's growing dictionary. I'll tell you, it's a hell of a way to get an education.

"Blessed are the meek, for they shall inherit the earth."
—Matthew 5:5

Chapter 41

Laquan is found

No matter how organized the librarian, it is the law of nature: things get disorganized. The fiction ends up on the shelf alongside the philosophers. The reference book sits next to the *Greatest Battles of World War II*. It's inevitable. Books move.

So do prisoners. From tier to tier. In and out of mental health. Back and forth between BMU (Behavior Management Unit). Depending on how tamed someone becomes when locked in and isolated twenty-three hours a day. They travel between their cells and the visitors' room, to and from our school. Across complexes into Building B and back to Building E, or the Satellite as the students call it.

All day long, a microphoned voice blares overhead, "Movement" and announces a group moving from one area to the next. Once or twice a day, a "Hold all movements" is sounded. And then everything just freezes. It's all like a clanging production line of human beings run on a conveyor belt moving from cell to cell, shower to cafeteria to rec yard. Every once in a while, the gears jam and the engines stop.

And then it starts again. The inmates' lives are mechanized. Their lives—no longer their own. All scheduled by the voice overhead.

So it's easy to get lost in the shuffle. To suddenly be sitting on the philosophy shelf when you're supposed to be in history.

So, it's even easier for our school to lose students. We get new students. We lose them. No one tells us when or why.

We don't get an advance ticket from the court, from the jail or even from an interested lawyer. No one tells us that "Johnny's going up top" or that "Shaquan's getting out." It all works rather informally.

You talk to the kid; he estimates his time or tells you what's going on. We act on that. If they're getting out, we try to set something up—reconnect with a school district or set something else up. If they're involved with the court, sometimes, they're mandated to a program instead. Or if they're going "up top." With them, it's easier. At least, we know where they're going and what they'll be doing.

When Laquan left, Janet and I were relieved that the court had worked out a program for him. With a 70 or less IQ and the emotional index of a five-year-old, he wasn't going to survive much longer in jail. The last we had seen him, we had given him his IEP—an Individualized Educational Program—a sort of punch list of his disabilities and the help that he needed because of them.

We had told him to give this IEP to "his friend," the social worker over at Legal Aid who was handing it over to Laquan's attorney to use in court. With the IEP in hand, the DA would have to understand. Hopefully, his charges could be lowered from a D felony to misdemeanors, and the social worker assured me that they were going to find him a program. Thank God!

That was about three months ago.

Today, Laquan's name popped up on our list. I almost thought he had caught a new charge. But it turns out, he's just been lingering in Building B. Sitting over on one shelf when he should be on another.

Misplaced.

With Laquan, that's pretty easy to do. He's a book with pretty worn edges. It's not clear if his father's ever been around, and Mrs. Sheridan is the only person present in his life right now. Who knows where his Mama went. Maybe his mother didn't understand how soft covered Laquan really was.

It's not clear where his mother is, but he's been living with Mrs. Sheridan, and Laquan isn't easy to live with. He's got a temper. And now that he's almost twenty and looks like a man, that temper can cause a lot of damage. Mrs. Sheridan can't walk too well, and she can't keep up with what's he's doing, but if he gets out, she'll let him stay. But she's worn out. A book ready to be replaced.

Nobody much noticed that Laquan was misplaced. That he hadn't been to court. That he hadn't seen a judge. Nobody much noticed.

And the longer no one noticed, and the longer Laquan sat on the shelf, the more he felt ready to explode. And he did. And he found himself in BMU—locked in all day. With no one to notice and no one to call.

Until he came back. When he told Janet where he'd been. And she told me.

"Laquan, have you seen your lawyer?" He shook his head.

"Your friend, the social worker?" Another back and forth motion. His thick glasses thrown once too many times across the room bounced off his ears as his head moved from side to side.

"Have you been to court?"

He smirked. Laquan often smirked. It conveyed a sense of attitude and shielded him against total vulnerability. But I suspected it also shouted things like smartaleck or punk to an unseasoned legal aid who relied on body language for the two-minute interview between clients.

So now, he smirked. "I ca, can't s, s, s … eee a judge. Only "ba, ba, El … el … pa … pen th, thera pee," stuttering out the phrase painfully.

He'd learn the jail lingo well. He had an uncanny ability to almost echo what his cellmates said—a common trait among special education students—something called echolalia. They can repeat the words, but they have no idea what they just said.

Two bolognas and a milk. The phrase for the transporting of inmates to court was commonplace. The boys sat in a holding cell all day. They saw court. They saw a judge. All they did was be transported "back home." Like the pitchers sitting out the game in the bullpen.

So had Laquan been sitting out his proceedings, or lack there in.

"Have you talked to anyone?" I strained to find someone who knew something besides Laquan.

He shook his head. He smirked. As if he didn't care when he did. He smirked, and I thought of the legal aid lawyer meeting him for the first time. Seeing that smirk that disguised the child. I thought of the legal aid who might be fooled into seeing a man instead of a child.

We sat for a few minutes more. And I saw, too, the child. The thick glasses. The crossed eyes. The bent head. The expressionless stare. The blank slate of incomprehension that only a teacher tries to write on.

The lawyer could only see Laquan's charges. The school, only his disability. And Laquan needed us to see both. There was no bridge to connect us together. No bridge that allowed us to talk. No court for the mentally disabled, only the mentally disturbed.

I walked Laquan back to the classroom and told Janet I'd try and reach Legal Aid.

Two emails and a voicemail later, the Legal Aid social worker, "Laquan's friend," wrote me that she would reach out to his attorney. She'd try to explain how little he understood. By yesterday, Laquan was convinced he was going upstate for two years after finally meeting with him.

"The lawyer said I'll have 200 days by the time I go to court next week, Mrs. Z," he appraised the situation.

Which equated to what? He hadn't been sentenced. He hadn't pled out. Had he even been indicted? Was there a legal implication for the 200? I had no idea. But neither really did he.

The people at school couldn't help. His absent family couldn't help. His lawyer couldn't help. He was misplaced. Forgotten.

Library shelves get organized. Eventually. Oddly, so do jails.

The most vulnerable, like Laquan, get shelved in the

wrong place—in jail. The number of mentally ill in prisons has almost quadrupled in the last decade—estimated at almost 20 percent of the jail population. Add to that, another 10 percent who had been homeless, and you have a lot of people who've been shelved in the wrong place. There are two to four times more mentally ill prisoners than there are mentally ill in the general population.

I don't know what got Laquan in BMU, but only the most serious assaults or acts of violence get you in there. Prisoners with mental illness find it more difficult to follow prison rules and to deal with the daily stresses of being locked up. They are more likely to break the rules, have a fight or be the victim of a fight.

And to make matters worse, they are often the ones who get punished because of the symptoms of their mental illness. They're defiant, or they're noisy. They're belligerent toward other inmates or are harmful to themselves. They end up being housed separately or like Laquan, put in isolating conditions that aggravate their conditions more.

There are a lot of Laquans in here. People without family. People without lawyers. People who've been misplaced. And forgotten. After awhile, they find themselves all sitting on the same shelf, and they don't want to leave because they've found each other. And they do it all by themselves, without any help, without the help of any system.

"I've learned that you can tell a lot about a person by the way(s) he handles these three things: a rainy day, lost luggage, and tangled Christmas tree lights."
—Maya Angelou

Chapter 42

Night School

It's Christmas.

With those words comes an explosion of memories and sensations. Without the accompanying sound. Without the sleigh bells ringing, jingling. Without the shoppers passing. Without the choirs singing. Without a bar of "White Christmas" being sung.

It's Christmas. The time of equinox. Our reptilian brains recognizing the passing of light. The mammalian brain wanting to defy it.

It's Christmas. And the boys know it. Know it without a trace of holiday surrounding them.

Nothing here much resembles Christmas but the month. December.

The same beige cinder block walls remain. Unadorned. No holly. No ivy. No tinsel. No lights. No Charlie Brown Christmas trees.

I'm teaching night school the day before Christmas Eve and feel the tension in the halls.

More boys are being sent to BMU. More guys are going to Ad Seg.

Skins are thin.

I announce that we'll be watching a movie instead of having class. I announce that we'll be watching a movie—of my choice. What might have become delight dissolves to "*ughs*."

"What's the movie, Mrs. Z? Why can't we just play games on the computers?"

I look over to Rasheed with a practiced teacher's glance.

"No computers. We're going to watch this movie. I love this movie." I smile. It takes years of being in a classroom to practice adamancy. I have it down pat.

Kenny moans, "What is it?"

"*The Christmas Story.*"

Rasheed grimaces. As if choreographing a dance, he executes six simultaneous grimaces in the other faces now occupying each seat.

Kenny asserts his dissent. "Why don't we have a vote?"

"You can vote with your feet, Kenny. Go or stay."

Nobody budges.

Rasheed is formidable though. "What are you trying to do, Mrs. Z? Make us depressed? We're stuck in here and you're going around showing us Christmas movies?"

I love their sarcasm. Their spirit. Their bravado. I wouldn't stand them down. That's what's landed many of them in here in the first place. Some adult "in charge" type who just had to have their moment of being in charge, of showing Rasheed who's the boss. Of pointing out the merits of his sitting through a movie he didn't want to sit through.

"You don't have to stay, Rasheed. But this movie is so stupid, it just makes me laugh out loud. I just thought that sitting where you are right now, you all need to laugh."

Nobody gets up. I push the play button.

They've seen the movie a hundred times before. Everyone has. Including me. It's a Christmas classic. A boy dreaming of getting a BB gun for Christmas. No different than dreaming of getting out of jail. I wonder what these young men had dreamed of when they did dream about Christmas.

Rasheed and Kenny are totally uninterested. They're in the back talking and being distractive. Carlos has taken a magazine and is flipping through the pages. I'm the only one watching, and I'm counting the minutes until my surrender. I might as well let them go on the computers.

Then one by one, they succumb to their dreams. There's laughter. And there's lightness. And it's almost as if we're no longer in jail. Well, almost.

This movie is all the gift I can bring. No candy canes readied for hooch. No cupcakes trafficked for sale. Everything is commodity here. As I've discovered already with my books.

As the movie unfolds and the boys joke about their Christmas tomorrow being no different from today, they don't realize that their laughter is gift.

They joke about the awful turkey dinner that is served—how turkey roll doesn't roll, it just lays flat, and how meager the portions. They talk about the dinners they'll miss. About the dinners they'll eat when they get out.

As they talk and joke and laugh, I find gratitude—in my crazy family that I'll be spending Christmas with. In the feast we'll be sharing—and even in Aunt Martha's Jell-O salad.

It's time to leave, and I wish them a Merry Christmas. Throw in a Happy New Year. I know that some of them will manage to find their way home during the holidays. I say a prayer that they won't find their way back.

As the CO outside the door calls their names, I call back to them, "See you all next year—or maybe, on line in CVS."

It takes a minute or two to compute, and it's met with seven broad smiles. "Yeah, Mrs. Z., see you next year or," they grin, "maybe, in CVS."

For lack of anything else to give, a laugh or two. Enough to get them through the week until we got back.

Truth is, I hoped that someday I'd meet them all on line in CVS. And that life would give them more to laugh about than it had up until now.

"Merry Christmas! Happy New Year!"

"If you want to know how many prison cells to build, look at the number of third graders who can't read."
—Sen. Mary Landrieu (D-LA)

Chapter 43

Tyshana's Son

All libraries have returned book stamps. That's where the term circulating comes from. The books go in and out. Even ebooks. In and out.

Unfortunately, the same principle holds true here. Except the term circulating is replaced by the word recidivism. Perpetual relapse. Not really in and out like those books. Every time somebody goes out and comes back in, it's five more steps backward, and five more and five more. Like digging a hole so deep that eventually, you can never get out.

My husband's home health aide arrived yesterday morning a few minutes late and very upset. Her son—the one who had been in jail, the one she just bailed out—was back in jail. Five steps backward.

He'd already spent two years upstate at a juvenile detention center. He'd already lost a football scholarship. He'd already lost the respect of most of his family.

Now he'd lost his chance for probation and now, Tyshana had lost $2,500 she had put up for bail—$2,500 she didn't have, making twelve dollars per hour.

She's typical of a lot of the families here—poor, black, and fed up with the in and out, with the steps backward. Sooner or later, Tyshana will get fed up enough not to put up bail money, not to believe that her son can move forward, not to believe that the system will help rehabilitate him.

In and out. Like library books, but Tyshana doesn't own a library card. Surprisingly, it turns out that Tyshana loves to read. She's borrowed my Nook and has been reading all the books I downloaded and haven't had the time to read. Besides, she loves to read to her grandbabies, as she calls them, before they go to bed.

Tyshana had her kids young—seventeen or eighteen. She never finished school and beats herself up that she didn't keep her son from being swallowed up by the streets, didn't read to him as she's doing to her grandbabies.

I keep telling her that the streets are very difficult to compete with. They are. If truth be told, she was swallowed up by them to begin with.

She's reading my books now. She's discussing them. There's no reason why she couldn't have been reading the same books I did when she was seventeen. She's bright. She's inquisitive. She's reflective. But the streets grabbed her, just as they've grabbed her son.

I'm not saying that a book or a library card would have empowered her to get out. An education certainly would.

And that's why I'm behind a book cart rolling down a short hallway in a jail. There are not a lot of us in this school, and there are an awful lot of "in and out" boys. We gotta believe that we're giving them three steps forward for every five steps back. And just one of these times, we're going to be ahead.

"But put two librarians' heads together,
and mountains move."
—Richard Peck, *Here Lies the Librarian*

Chapter 44

Addy

My book cart has become one of the most inspirational things in my life. Nothing has given me so much satisfaction, but it shouldn't surprise me. I think I've had this Walter Mitty life of being a librarian my whole life. Besides, no matter what school I've been in, the librarians have always been my people of choice. The librarians are my favorite people, and the library my favorite haunt. So it's no surprise that when given the chance to add a sidebar to my job description—librarian would be right on top of the list.

Knowing all those librarians—well, what do they say about knowing people at the top? Once I got started, I knew all the right people to ask—well, to beg—for what I wanted: Donna at East Meadow High School for the cart; Anne at the other high school, Clarke, for card jackets; and the folks in the Prison Librarian's Group to add a few more donations to the collection we already had. It all kind of snowballed since then. And it all has become tremendously good.

People, not just the librarians, are interested in our library cart. People, not just librarians, care about whether our students have books. It's not just me that thinks it's a good idea that seventeen-year-olds and eighteen- and nineteen-year-olds without an education and sitting in jail try to get a GED and read a book or two while they're sitting here. Odd, but most people, not just librarians, or the teachers here, think that these kids should be given a second chance.

We are a people of second chances. We like to rally round the slumped Rocky and cheer for him to rise.

Once I start talking about our library cart, people are cleaning off their book shelves and donating books. They want to be a part of these kids' second chances.

"I have a bunch of books I can give you. Do you think they'd like a biography on Michael Jordan?"

I sometimes imagine all of those people with all of those books showing as much interest when my guys weren't here. When they were still out on the street. Pointing them toward Barnes & Noble. Or toward the library. When they were little boys.

Donating a book is easy. Donating time is not.

Addy shows up at night school carrying a pile of books. He's had them out for weeks and, truthfully, I didn't expect to get them back. Word's out that he's been "state-ready"—sentenced, and processed for transport to an upstate prison. It's just a matter of time before he goes.

He's taken care of all the preliminary details of his exit. His head is shaved. The long dreads he's sported and weaved are gone. It's either shave them here or when he gets there. He's given his stuff away: he'll leave with the bright orange clothes on his back. The rest, given to friends. No chance on getting it back to property. Most books, thrown in a community pile—at least they'll be read. Addy has some shred of responsibility left. He needs to bring those books back to me. He's been so shredded that there's almost nothing else left to give. I respect the remnants of the young man in front of me.

"Wow, Addy. Thank you."

"No problem, Mrs. Z. I wanted to make sure I got them back. I'm leaving tomorrow."

There's a note of sadness in his voice, a need to say good-bye when good-byes aren't allowed because there are too many of them.

I take the books and put them back on the cart. Alphabetically. Modeling my librarian friends. Putting my index cards back into the pocket jackets. Recreating some kind of ordered accountability. Giving Addy credits for bringing them back. Giving my catalog enough characterization to make it fiction.

So my library cart has become an inspiration—a symbol. For me. For the boys. For my librarian friends. For the people who want to donate books.

It's created many connections.

But Addy emphasizes its smallness. How empty it can become. How squeaky its wheels. How limited are our halls.

It is only three wooden shelves high—two-sided and divided by language, English and Spanish. A bilingual community on wheels. But those books can't travel too far. From the school to the dorms. They are not state-ready, and they can't go to Ad Seg or BMU. If you're alone, then you sit alone. Without the company of a book.

So my library connections can only travel so far, too.

My friend Anne, over at the high school, became one

of our benefactors. We are the recipients of World Book Night. Through her, a publisher donates thirty copies of a book as a gift. What a treasure. Only trouble is for a lot of boys, it can't make it beyond our gates. Forget inspirational inscriptions. Forget the touchstone of something positive in one's life. Ideas are as limited as dreams here.

"See if they have any college courses when you get settled upstate, Addy." I encourage him. He's already passed the GED. On the outside, he'd have applied to college. He could still have that chance, or at least begin.

And I hang on to that thought today. Because I am beginning to realize that hope is a chain reaction and that the reason that book cart is so important to me isn't because I like to sign out books and control them coming back.

The reason people are so willing to donate a book or two, and the reason Anne and Donna help me out, and why Mary Robinson over at Nassau Library or Renée McGrath does is because, even though Addy is still going upstate, he's still nineteen, and he's still got a chance of getting out of the cycle of despair he's been spinning on. He still has hope.

And books capture that hope.

Oh, I don't expect the boys to see that.

"Hey, Mrs. Z, do you have any Harry Potters?" When they asked, they never saw hope in their question. I did.

There was the hope that they had the innocence of children in them still.

When they ask for a James Patterson or Stuart Woods, there's hope. I've never heard of one of them that doesn't applaud Alex Cross. They aren't cheering the villain—no matter how much they pretend to be one or, unfortunately, have chosen to act like one.

No matter the book, there's always hope. The hope that reading will help us transcend whatever drags us down.

"I'm gonna study, Mrs. Z," Addy said as assuringly as he had said, "I'll be in early, Ma," on the night of his arrest. And just to make me feel better, he added, "I'm not gonna do nothing to get me in trouble up there. I promise." And I hoped he wouldn't.

I wished he could put a book in his pocket. Some hope. Maybe, just a quote. Something from Benjamin Franklin or Martin Luther King, Jr. Maybe just a note. How about: *Read. Be free.* And *hope.* (*God speed, Addy*).

"The best way to find yourself is to lose yourself in the service of others."
—Mahatma Gandhi

Chapter 45

Mary, The Lady from the Library

I always liked books with happy endings. Movies, too. "A Midsummer Night's Dream" over "Hamlet."

Corny, feel-good endings instead of tearjerkers. Not too many of those around here.

Interestingly, the boys liked those, too. Well, not corny. But books that ended on a positive note. Happy endings. Kids messed up with gangs who somehow escaped. Street kids who did time and got out—and didn't go back. Books about lives that clung onto life as tenaciously as they hung onto hope. Those were the kind of books they were willing to pick up and read. Well, were willing to try—with the right book jacket and the right title.

Immortal ... The Barrio Kings ... Rikers High ...

I actually discovered the Top Ten List of Books for Incarcerated Teens. And not in *The New York Times*. I tripped over it—via the library (of course!).

All stories have their good guys and their bad guys. And jail has its share of both.

Every human being is a story.

Each, a tale to tell. Inmate, CO, teacher, jail cook—there is no difference. There is a story in each of us. And each have a story to tell.

My students needed theirs to be shouted.

And when Mary Robinson, Outreach Services director at the Nassau Library Systems, entered their lives, she handed them a megaphone.

I had gotten her name and number from a CO weeks before. CO Myers had been the jail's one point of contact with the public library. No education background. No library degree. Just a love of books. And a gut instinct that reading and education did these kids some good. And the good sense that books and school might be these kids' ticket out.

I was stacking books when Myers approached me. "You know, you should contact Mary Robinson at the Nassau Library System?"

I'll admit it now. My own busyness was remiss.

A few weeks later, my desk phone rang. "This is Mary Robinson, the new Outreach director at the Nassau Library System. CO Myers gave me your name."

And we talked. For almost an hour.

We talked about the kids here, about the kind of books they liked. She was very surprised to find out that they were reading books.

She was even more surprised to find that there weren't really many books to read. What constituted the public library's idea of circulating, and that of the jail's, had become an empty hole: books being dropped here and everywhere.

We talked about "my boys," the youngest ones, being locked up—to her surprise—almost twenty-four hours a day. With books being the only thing to do while shipwrecked on this island. And how important books were to almost everyone else when there wasn't much else left to do.

Then we met, and I got that list, some new books, and a new friend.

But if my library cart was only about books, all I'd need was the money to purchase more books. Those books and the ones that Mary was helping me get—they were giving shape to the stories that my students were yet to tell.

Their stories were yet incomplete, and those books were yet to give shape to tragedy or comedy.

A few weeks later, I invited Mary to come to the jail. The distance between my students' requests for books and their faces was far too great a space. She needed to take that trip.

It wasn't difficult to introduce her. Mary is a large black woman whose warmth precedes her. First, you notice a smile. Then, you notice Mary. Her magnetism wasn't weakened by her initial anxiety.

She nervously began to visit each classroom, carrying a yellow legal pad and a pencil. Her usually generous smile was a bit thin, but her natural friendliness compensated for it.

"This is Ms. Robinson, the lady I told you about from the Nassau Library."

The boys seemed impressed. I had told them that a "lady from the library" would be coming to take their requests. I don't think they had really believed me.

They seemed awestruck. Here was someone who was actually listening to their requests. They were sitting in a place where they no longer had the luxury of requests.

"Why don't you tell Ms. Robinson the books you'd like her to bring? I know you have quite a few requests."

Now, I was awestruck. The usually boisterous group of hooligans shouting, "Do you have a Stuart Woods?" "How about books on Greek mythology?," "Any books on overthrowing the government?" Then, they sat in an eerie silence.

Silence and nervousness. There was absolute quiet.

My thought: *How do I fill up this space?*

Now, I had to coax them to speak. The boys and Mary.

"Malcolm, didn't you want a book about Egyptian art?"

"Yeah, yeah, and books about drawing, how to draw things."

Mary jotted it down on her legal pad.

"David, what kind of books were you looking for?"

David, who never, ever shut up, stumbled. "Uh, uh, maybe an encyclopedia."

Mary didn't miss a beat. She didn't diminish any of their requests. She respected whatever they asked.

"How 'bout hood books, miss?"

And I heard Mary say, "Sure, we can work on getting you some of that ... "

Suddenly, she had made many friends, and we had gotten many new books.

But more than that, my boys had gotten some dignity restored. In that simple gesture. By being listened to.

It was like being on that shipwrecked island and finding a radio and yelling, "Help!" They had received a transmission back.

Mary started making suggestions. They started making more requests. There began a lively exchange.

When I walked Mary back through the gates and metal detectors and said good-bye, her legal pad was full.

Full of requests, yes. But full of something more. Full of the stories they told. Not in books printed and bound. Full of their own voice. Their own choice. If only in asking for something, one thing, they wanted, and being able to get it back. In a borrowed library book. Not in something to own. But in a loan. From the public library. But in their own choice.

Mary would have no way of understanding the power she had given them. Choices. In a dark space with none, not few. In a space where every morning, every day, every night, your every action, your every movement, is never a choice for you. Choices. A powerful thing.

A visit from the "lady from the library."

Maybe not a perfect happy ending. But the stuff that happy endings are made of.

"Nothing stops a bullet like a job."
—Homeboy Industries motto, Los Angeles

Chapter 46

Derik

Libraries are more than just a warehouse for books. When I was a kid, I loved to sit at the round tables in the children's room and do my homework after school. It felt so scholarly, as opposed to our dining room table alternative.

Today, the possibilities abound.

About a week after Derik was released, I gave him a call. My usual "I'll give you a week and then see if you did what you were supposed to do" call. Instead of Derik, I got his mother.

"Hi, Mrs. Ricken?" I introduced myself, explaining that I was following up on Derik about his finding a GED program.

Mrs. Ricken was very, very interested in GED programs for Derik. She was very, very interested in any programs for Derik. Any program that might keep Derik from coming back to jail again. He'd been here a couple of times before.

Her biggest trouble—as is mine—was getting Derik interested in finding one.

"No, no, we haven't found one," she stammered over the phone. "Do you know where we can find one?"

Now, Derik isn't from our county. He apparently decided to cross county lines to commit his crime. He's gone home but his probation officer and weekly visits stay right here in Nassau County, probably 75 miles, a $9.50 train fare or four bus transfers away. Neither Derik nor his mother own a car. I can't remember if he had stolen one.

So Derik is up against it to begin with. He has to show up at probation every week, or he'll be in violation. So whatever he pled to get himself out of here doesn't much matter if he misses that one appointment. And Mrs. Ricken knows it.

Six months, five years' probation sounded real good to Derik when he was sitting in here.

"I know I can be good, Mrs. Z. Stay out of trouble." They all tell me that. Every single day.

And in my greatest effort not to give legal advice, I tell them that when I was nineteen, EVEN "I" associated with people who were not always doing the right thing, and that's all they had to do to break probation.

All they had to do was stand next to someone not doing the right thing. That's not too difficult when you live on Terrace Avenue in Hempstead, or you go to school in Roosevelt, or you're walking down the street in Westbury.

Those are just towns and places I know about. Wherever it was Derik was, it was pretty much the same thing. Except he was likely to be picked up by his county's police for violating our county's probation.

Mrs. Ricken knew that. She needed him to get his GED. Right now, Derik didn't have his GED. He wasn't going back to school—he was too many credits short and too many years old. And without it, he wasn't going to get a decent job.

I really didn't know anything about programs there. I didn't know Mrs. Ricken; but I knew the urgency that I heard in her voice, that cry for help for her child that she'd been asking for over and over again. The doors she'd been knocking on. The ones probably never answered.

Derik was up against it because of his choices. His mother was up against it because she saw her son using up all of his options. She knew he had very few left, and he was only twenty years old.

"Derik said he only had one exam left, and he could graduate." She seemed a little relieved, even though she knew it couldn't be true. (It wasn't).

"No, he needs a lot more credits than that. It would be better if he got his GED. But he should be able to take the classes for free."

She seemed genuinely surprised. Almost relieved. As if Derik had never mentioned this. I know I gave him some information before he left.

"You can go to your local library—they'll give you information."

I don't know why I hadn't thought of it sooner. I'd been sending guys to the Department of Labor, to town and county agencies, to nonprofits, to you name it, and I had forgotten about that place with the round tables and all those reference books.

I was going to give Mrs. Ricken a call back—just to see if she had followed up.

This morning, I got my list of new enrollees, and I walked down to room 4 to say hello to Derik.

Turns out he did find a GED class and his mother did go to the library. Derik missed two probation appointments, though, and they picked him up riding in the backseat of his friend's car. His friend didn't have a license, ran a stop sign, and had some marijuana on him. He wasn't even arraigned.

Derik is going to have to wait a while to take the GED.

"We love those whom we serve."
—Richard Paul Evans, *The Christmas Box Miracle*

Chapter 47

Reaching Out

It's too bad that Derek went back to jail. He wasn't alone. More than four in ten offenders returned to state prison within three years of their release, and more than half of these offenders had failed to get a job upon their return to the community.

The library wasn't such a bad place for Derek to start looking for a job or to get his GED. One of the things that attracted me to studying library science wasn't that I was so keen on organizing and shelving books, but I was interested in the nation's public libraries' focus on Outreach Services, helping the underserved to access library and information services. It was to help people like Derek who more than likely were not going to the library for help, would never think of going to the library for help, and probably could find a lot of help there.

Right now, over nine million prisoners are released back to their communities each year, and that number is expected to increase as states and cities try to depopulate overcrowded prisons and create alternatives to incarceration. Almost 25 percent are being released without any form of community correctional supervision: without educational support or vocational training or job placement. Like Mrs. Ricken, they or their families are at their wits' end as to where to go to get some.

During my initial interview with the boys, I tell them, yes, that they can finish their high school diploma with us or get their GED, but the most important job I have is to sit and plan what they're going to do AFTER they're in jail. Now, for some of them, that's not possible. If you're going to spend the next two years upstate, it's premature to talk about what you'll be doing two months from now, but for the others, it IS the most important part of my job. Recidivism is just too high. If they're not connected with their family and community when they are released, they don't have a chance of not reoffending.

One of the biggest problems with the current economy isn't necessarily unemployment. Job competition is a big issue for these boys when they're released. The jobs that they used to be able to get with their limited educations are being taken by those with better educations who can't secure positions in their fields and are working two and three low-paying jobs and boxing our boys out.

These boys need the chance to home in on their skills, to reconnect with the technological advances in society that they've missed out on. I think the more academic term would be "to reintegrate." The public library offers them that opportunity. When we talk about alternatives to incarceration, libraries are rarely mentioned. They aren't a place of confinement, but they are a place of empowerment where the individual can help avoid being reincarcerated again.

The public library offers ex-offenders more than just access to books and magazines. They are often offered services that they cannot afford: computers, job training, and literacy programs like the GED program I mentioned to Mrs. Ricken.

Because it probably services one of the largest populations of ex-offenders as well as prisoners, the New York Public Library excels in its delivery of services to this population. It offers invaluable resources to ex-offenders by offering a guide of agencies and organizations, which are available for them to contact for services like housing or drug treatment or job training. Obviously, each public locality mightn't be able to create its own guide, but the librarians on staff might be able to become knowledgeable about local services and offer information to the ex-offenders in the community.

The American Library Association welcomes my boys. That's what they need when they're released—to be welcomed home. Their families do, but their schools look upon them as troublemakers, so the boys often don't want to go back. Then it's difficult to find a job or to pursue a GED. I try to tell them that their public library is a welcoming place. They rarely believe me either, because they haven't been there or if they have, it hadn't been such a welcoming place.

So I tell Derek, and I tell some of the others. And Mary Robinson becomes a "welcome mat." And maybe, our little rolling cart will be the positive connection that will help frame that future link. And maybe they'll find their library as an alternative. Maybe they'll find their library as a better choice than the ones they made before.

Most of all, maybe, they'll find that some librarian will make them feel more included, and they won't feel, as librarian Brendan Dowling, expressed it, like "ostracized members of society" anymore.

"I believe in prayer. It's the best way we have to draw strength from heaven."
—Josephine Baker

Chapter 48

David, Barney, and Wesley

One of the dangers of a jail library is kites—pieces of paper with messages or codes or pictures that are passed from one inmate to another. They can be passed in a million different ways, but books are as common as carrier pigeons. So I'm concerned when I see three pieces of folded paper lying on my desk one morning. I'm certain it's the kiss of death for our library. I ready myself for the sergeant to shut us down. Instead, when I open them, I find notes from three of the night school guys—David, Barney, and Wesley—all asking "a favor," hand-delivered by Mrs. K. David, as usual, is trying to track down his family. He's getting state-ready. He expects to be sent upstate in three weeks, and no one is answering the phone. He wants his stuff picked up and sent home. Or it will be thrown away. He wants his stuff—his pages and pages of rap music that I know he's written. That I know he's going to publish and get famous for. The drawings that he etched. The photographs his girlfriend (now a heartache) sent. He needs his stuff.

****** KITE #1

Ask my sister why she won't pick up the phone when there's money still on it. Tell her to please pick up the phone before I go upstate. Please and thank you, Ms. Z ... Ruby Gautier 718 707 5930 (1-347-688-9217)

****** KITE #2

MOM can you come up to the jail Friday and put money on my books please. Charles, Barney (1-347-248-0262)

(No mincing words. He needs what he needs. Trouble is he's not likely to get it)

****** KITE #3

(Mom) Nancy Tell my mom that Im okay. Tell her I love her. Tell her Im thankful for everything. Tell her to stay strong. And pray. Wesley Kolk

And that's how I began my day. Thinking about David, Barney, and Wesley, and about their moms. Not knowing anything about their moms and knowing everything about them. Wanting to tell them to pray. Knowing that was the only thing that could do. David's mom didn't pick up the phone; on Barney's I left a voice message; Wesley's mom picked up. I fumbled over the beginning of our conversation. How was I going to summarize Wesley's note. "You know, Ms. Kolk, let me just read you the note he left—it makes it much simpler." And I read his note aloud.

There was a quiet pause before Ms. Kolk spoke. "You know, Ms. Zeman, you tell Wesley not to worry about my being strong. I'm fine. Tell him to be strong. And we'll both pray."

"I'll make sure to tell him, Ms. Kolk. He'll be glad I got through to you."

"You tell him that I love 'im, too," and she paused, "'cause I do love him, even if he got himself in some trouble."

I understood. I really did. "You know, Ms. Kolk, my husband passed when I was forty, and my two boys took it very badly. They were in seventh and ninth grade, and they gave me a run for my money after." I paused. "They got in some trouble, too."

That seemed such a long time ago. Sometimes, I shared that with mothers, sometimes not. My boys had gotten in some trouble when my first husband died, and they had given me a real hard time. It was a very painful time of our lives, and I wouldn't wish that on anyone. "It was worse than my husband dying."

And it was. It WAS a very painful time, and there was a lot of time and distance between now and then. It was always difficult to go back there again.

"But the good news is that now they are both very successful young men. I tell that to the boys all the time. You make some mistakes. It's human to make mistakes. You don't have to repeat the same mistakes all over again."

When I talk about it, I know that I made mistakes. There are some things that I regret that I did back then with my sons. I mightn't do it that way today. I can't change one thing today that I did yesterday. But I can make changes today. I'm sure that Ms. Kolk and Ms. Charles and Ms. Gautier have made mistakes. All of us. The boys. The mothers. The fathers. If we had to do it all over again, well, maybe we'd do it all differently.

Since our lives aren't written with a lead pencil, they can't be erased so easily. But they can change. "I'll tell Wesley to be strong, Ms. Kolk," and added, "and to pray."

If Wesley or Ms. Kolk or I were going to change at all, we all needed a little extra help from above. Jail is a place full of people who've made mistakes, but the world is, too. We can learn from our mistakes. And we can turn those mistakes into blessings—when we share them with others. *Amen.*

"Wisdom ... is knowing what you have to accept."
—Wallace Stegner

Chapter 49

Hector's Gift

Mary Robinson's order came through. She called me up and asked me to come over to the Nassau Library System and pick up two box loads of books.

She had made some great choices. Some, of course, we had discussed. *I Am Four* followed by *The Power of Six*. Very popular and shaken right off our library shelf. I had no more copies left.

But there were some she slid in that I had to leave to her expertise and experience. After all, she had both the time and the energy to peruse the library journals and book reviews. I didn't. And the books she had chosen did look interesting: *The History of Africa, The African-American Almanac, Hot Salsa: Bilingual Poems,* and *Victor Cruz,* a Spanish edition of his biography. I hoped all would hit our top ten list. I was already strategizing a marketing campaign as I helped her load the boxes into my car.

"Thanks, Mary. I am sure the boys are going to love these."

Mary giggled. It reinforced her goodness and gentleness. I really liked her. Outreach Services covered a huge territory—certainly, not one that I'd ever attempt to serve, but if anyone was up to the challenge, she was.

She giggled again, "I hope they like these. I didn't really know exactly what they'd like. But I hope I chose selections that match their interests."

I loved her librarian-speak. I was hanging around the boys too much. I was immersed in "ya got," and "this ain't what I want," and "don't ya have any hood books?" too much, instead of discussing selections and interest levels.

Just as we loaded the last box in the car, one book fell on the ground, and Mary bent to pick it up.

"Oh, you know, I don't know if anyone would be interested in these, but I put in a few books on sketching—and urban drawings ... they looked pretty good. Especially for anyone with an interest in drawing or art."

She held up a book with a beautifully designed and detailed front cover that reminded me of that somewhat geometric looking sketch of Leonardo da Vinci's "Vitruvian Man."

"I know a lot of the boys will be interested, Mary. Thanks."

I did know a lot of them were interested in drawing and sketching and painting and tattooing and art.

They were always asking me to get them copies of cartoon characters to copy or Celtic designs.

They were always asking me if we had any pens.

I have a carefully folded drawing tucked inside my pocketbook. Two bent hands clasped in prayer, rosary beads and a heart. Sketched in black ink on a ripped sheet, the only drawing paper available. Alongside it the Serenity Prayer—in Spanish—and a note of thanks.

Señor,
dame la Serenidad necesaria para aceptar las cosas
que no puedo cambiar.
Coraje para cambiar las
cosas que puedo,
y Astucia para saber la diferencia
entre ellas.
Muchas gracias, Señor

About a year ago, Hector gave it to me, and I've carried it with me ever since. Not only to remember him, but to remember why I stay at this job every day when sometimes so little changes.

I cherish the calligraphy letters so carefully inked onto the unraveling threads of a discolored white sheet, his easel. The only easel allowed him. The black ink squeezed from one of the jail's regulation stubby plastic pens, inch by inch, drop by drop—one of the reasons our pens are the commodity they are.

Last week, one of our newer visitors was quick to observe.

"Ya know, Mrs. Z, when I was at Rikers, we had art class. Why don't we have art class here?"

"I don't know, Manuel." I really didn't know. I really didn't know why we couldn't have magic markers or paint or colored pencils. Or at least some kind of compromise position.

I really didn't know how it was all about security here when it wasn't about security somewhere else. It's a funny thing about working in jail; you're following the rules just like everybody else. Like them or not. It's one of the realities: Everyone relinquishes some part of his freedom when he enters through those doors.

What was it that Dante said? "Abandon hope, all ye who enter here." And he begins his descent into Hell.

Here, the gates close behind you—worker or inmate. Crash. You abide by rules. Their rules, rules that mightn't have rhyme or reason, but you don't ask why. For inmates, certainly not.

I'm certainly not asking about crayons. As my mother would say, "There's bigger fish to fry."

So there are art classes there and not here. But there's nothing but time at a lot of others.

Be grateful for what you got. Pay attention to the rules. Don't question anything aloud.

Nothing is uniform except the axiom: You gotta pay attention to the rules. Once you pass through those gates, abandon everything, abandon who you are, abandon dignity, abandon every shred of who and what you thought you were.

For a couple of hours a day, I pay attention. I don't question anything aloud. Just like everybody else, I follow the rules and process everything inside and then leave and let everything explode into these printed words.

If I could, I'd draw or sketch—maybe have it explode in bursts of paint or ink.

As I drive back toward the jail with the boxes of books that Mary's put in the back of my car, I keep thinking of the boys who like to draw and sketch and those art books she's put in the box.

And how their thoughts might explode in bursts of color instead of the blood that the COs often see splayed across the cement floor.

I'm thinking about Hector's folded scrap in my pocketbook: *Señor, dame la Serenidad necesaria para aceptar* ... (Lord, grant me the serenity to accept ...)

Then Jesus told this parable:
"A man had a fig tree planted in his vineyard, and he
went to look for fruit on it, but did not find any. So he
said to the man who took care of the vineyard, 'For three
years now I've been coming to look for fruit on this fig
tree and haven't found any. Cut it down! Why should it
use up the soil?' 'Sir,' the man replied, 'leave it alone for
one more year, and I'll dig around it and fertilize it. If it
bears fruit next year, fine! If not, then cut it down.'"
Luke 13:6–9

Chapter 50

Hope Whispers

Salim comes to night school and declares he has two weeks left. He wants information on college.

"But you haven't been sentenced yet, have you?" I am wary of jumping the gun. I know he can't pay for school, and his felony bars him from getting his financial aid back. But I don't want to curb his enthusiasm.

"My sentencing date is in two weeks, and I've pled out to two years." He smiles a rather broad and winsome smile. He smiles the same teacher-to-pupil smile that I used to smile right before any lesson on punctuation. "I've already served eighteen months, waiting for my case to go to court, Mrs. Z." He sighed. "That means time served— I'm out."

I hope it's true.

Hope is so elusive here. Hidden. As well she should be. Fragile, gentle, and beautiful things do not survive.

David is lucky he has. He was at night school last night. It was good to see him again. There he was—all six-foot-three of him tangling out of his chair.

"They haven't called me up to school, Mrs. Z. I went

ahead and got my GED and then, wham, they stopped calling me."

My wish for David, a college degree.

We're watching a movie, and the pilot taking flight. The plane soars through thick clouds, and the plane rumbles and shakes. The instrument panel lights as thunderclaps around the cockpit.

"Is that really what it's like?" David trembles in his seat next to my desk. "I don't think I'm ever going to ride in a plane."

I wish him a smooth first flight somewhere sunny. Beyond Far Rockaway.

Those books on my cart keep Hope alive. Those books, the repeated titles never returned, repeat Hope's name not Despair's. There's good reason they never come back. All inmates in all jails cling to Hope.

Hope whispers that desire to change. She says, "I'm not going to do this again." Hope plants the seed to change.

Some of these boys needn't have been locked up to hear her call his name. I can't help but think there might have been other ways. My book cart and how they respond tell me that there are other ways. That book cart has given me Hope, and she has called my name.

"And the most important part of my job," as I tell each boy who first sits in front of my desk … is to "help you" get back in school, get home, maybe find a job," because most guys agree this is not the best five star hotel they ever stay at." Rehearsed, yes, but true.

Always the same nervous laugh follows. Almost the same identical response, "Yeah, I'm not coming back here ever again." And I hope he never does.

It's Reality that gets in the way. And in the way and in the way.

David remains wingless. Salim can't get a start. Rasheed too much the hustler to change. Laquan too much the resident here to move.

We're still in the room watching "Flight." A doped-up and drunk pilot manages successfully to fly an airplane upside down and land it with few fatalities. And a slick lawyer is about to get him off. His only problem: conscience. All he has to do is put the blame on his dead girlfriend, the flight attendant onboard.

He's called before a commission to testify. He's doing fine. Keeping his cool. Doing exactly what the lawyer's said. Until he has to link his girlfriend to the one piece of incriminating evidence against him—an airline-size bottle of booze. He confesses instead. He realizes that the truth is more powerful than lies. He realizes that the truth is his freedom.

David jumps out of his seat, "I can't believe it. What a jerk: I hate this movie." He grumbles as he gets up to leave. "Mrs. Z, I really liked this movie until the end. The ending ruined the whole thing."

The other five boys in the room respond. Without my saying anything. Each one of them comments on David's outburst.

"He had to live with himself. He'd go out and kill himself by getting high if he didn't tell the truth." Kasim's assessment.

Jorim inserts his observation: "He'd be a coward to hang it on the dead woman: she saved that little boy. She was really a hero."

David protests. He's still disgruntled. Uncertain but listening.

I hear Hope whispering.

As they get up to leave the room, I turn to David. "Think about the ending and let me know what you think next week."

This morning, I called Leadership Training Institute to make a referral, and they told me Jakaan had been showing up every day to study for his GED. I had referred at least ten boys to LTI in the last two months. Jakaan had been the only one who showed up.

"Thanks, Donna. It's good to know."

It was good to know. If Jakaan showed up, so could Donald or Salim or Adriel or Taquan or Josiah or …

Hope did exist—she wandered throughout their lives. And they had something else:

Youth and possibility.

"True life is lived when tiny changes occur."
—Leo Tolstoy

Chapter 51

Sister Dolores

Sister Dolores and I sometimes like to stack the deck. I think you call that cheating, but I figure when you're in cahoots with a Roman Catholic nun, the eternal consequences aren't going to be so bad.

So every once in a while, we stick a book or two in between the John Grishams and James Pattersons—the Library of Congress classified suspense thrillers—and sneak in books labeled "inspirational fiction." Like mixing baby aspirin in applesauce. The boys barely notice it.

So, of course, I am always trying to sneak those books onto the cart. When the boys wander up and there's almost nothing left of the Pattersons and Woods and Grishams, and when the comics are gone and there's nothing left, I reach for one of those books and ever so gently suggest. And when there's almost nothing else left in the world to read. Well, when there's almost nothing else in the world to do, well …

And when Menelik comes to school his first day, the cart is almost bare. He's bright and bored. A lethal combination on the outside. In here, though, a combination that, with a push in the right direction, CAN produce more positive effects.

Menelik's mother had worked very hard at keeping him out of here. Almost. She had taken him from Brownsville and shipped him off to Baldwin—a seemingly safer place—to finish his senior year. Only two months more, and he'd be home free.

Well, almost.

There was only one problem: Menelik. He took Menelik with him no matter where he'd go. There was still that vacant house calling to him to be broken into. There was still that window waiting to be smashed.

When he got up out of his seat to look through the cart, there was practically nothing there.

"Don't you got anything good to read?"

I volleyed back. "How do you define good"?

"Ya' know—hood books, books about the streets, things like that."

There was nothing mildly resembling "good" on the cart.

I picked up a few books and made suggestions. "Here's an autobiography," or "You might like this one about sports trivia—a lot of guys like it. It's a good read in your cell." Nothing grabbed his attention. He left empty-handed.

Menelik was bright, bored, and had attitude. He wasn't going to concede that he was interested in anything that I offered. I'd have to wait for the boredom to really set in.

I called his high school counselor. His mother wasn't the only one who was devastated.

Ms. Obayemi sounded distraught when I told her who I was and where Menelik was.

"He was doing so well ..." Her voice trailed off. I could tell she had suffered a lot of disappointments sitting at her desk.

"Well, Menelik said he was almost finished all his credits, so I thought maybe we could coordinate something with his teachers so that he could still graduate on time." A GED wasn't always the only option. Not when he was this close.

We spoke a little. Ms. Obayemi was young, idealistic, and hopeful. All of the things that someone like Menelik needed in a guidance counselor. Someone to believe in him. And Ms. Obayemi did. Bless her soul.

She interrupted, "Would I be able to visit Menelik?"

I really didn't know. No teacher or guidance counselor had ever bothered to ask. No one seemed that invested in any of these students. I wasn't going to discourage someone who actually was.

"Well, I know you can visit, but let's try and arrange a classroom visit at the school rather than your visiting in the visitor's room."

A week later, Ms. Obayemi and a coworker were sitting in my office/classroom 5 with me chaperoning in the back—trying to give them as much privacy as reading the newspaper would allow.

I read the Macy's ads, and they talked. About the kids in Menelik's class. About the teachers. About the big baseball game he had missed. About the girl he liked. Messages he got from the other kids.

Then Ms. Obayemi asked the obvious. "So, what do you do with yourself all day?" Obvious but naive. A silly question to ask a seventeen-year-old who is locked in a cell all day.

"Well, I come to school in the morning, and I read a lot." He paused. "There's nothing else to do—I'm locked in all day."

Ms. Obayemi looked embarrassed for asking. But she quickly regained her momentum. "What kind of things do you like to read?"

"Well, mysteries and stuff. I read a lot of James Patterson ... and Stuart Woods."

I noticed Macy's was having a sale.

Menelik rambled on, "and like I was reading this book last night—it's called *The Shack*. You wouldn't believe this book, Ms. O. There was something about this book."

I stopped worrying about the shoes at Macy's. Menelik got my attention. I wondered how he had gotten that book. I knew he hadn't signed it out from the cart. My copies had all walked and had never come back. Sister Dolores and I were just waiting to order more.

"I was reading this book and, I don't know, something about it made me fall to my knees. There was something very spiritual about the book. I just felt like I should pray."

Ms. Obayemi just said, "Wow."

I, too, wanted to jump up and yell Wow! I wanted to run out of the room and call Sister Dolores. I wanted to tell her that one of our feel-good books that we stuck between the "shoot 'em down deads" had won. A book about forgiveness, forgiving others, and forgiving ourselves, had triumphed over seeking revenge. *Amen!*

Menelik continued. Both Ms. Obayemi and I entranced. "And then the CO came down the hall and banged on my hut. He screamed, 'What are you doing down there on the floor?'" He paused. "What did he think I was doing?"

And then, Menelik stopped talking.

Nature changes slowly and quietly. The spring blossom doesn't just burst forth. In early March's frost, you see the faintest green bristles pushing through winter's gray bark. Day after day, they push and scratch and struggle to change. April finds buds. May, flowers.

What we see, what we hear, what we read—all nurture our growth. We push and scratch to change as slowly and quietly.

But it's really a struggle in this very dark place.

"It is easier to build strong children than to repair broken men."
—Frederick Douglass

Chapter 52

Boys with Blank Pages

Almost every book I read when I was a child ended with "and they all lived happily ever after." And that's the way I'd like it to be now, too. Obviously, it isn't—especially here. But the hope for happy endings is threaded into almost every boy who enters my life. That's what keeps me working with them, even when all they see are blank pages.

And this odd assortment of boys changes me.

As life always does, things change. Seasons change. Some things don't change. Some things will never change. Or they seem not to.

Some things in my life have. Some have not.

Michael came home. His infections went away—for now. Little by slowly, he's learning to walk. He'll never walk the same. His life will never be the same again. Our lives will never be the same again. It's changed.

I haven't won the lottery. I still have lots of hospital bills and a lot of credit card debt. That hasn't changed.

That's life.

Some of the boys' lives have changed. For the better. Some have not.

Jakaan is going to LTI every day and studying for his GED. Mario went back to college.

But David left for two years upstate, and Kourtney's back again. Changes, yes, but not for the better. For them, there haven't been any happy endings.

Now. But maybe tomorrow. Or tomorrow. There's always tomorrow.

"For with God, all things are possible."

I want to write a happy ending for each one of those boys. But know they need to write their own. Their books have not yet been bound.

Boys with blank pages. Waiting for happy endings. Waiting to see how their stories might be started all over again.

I wish I could write a happy ending. I want to take each one of these boys and create a new life for him. Have him turn this one around—go back to school, graduate. Apply to college. Become a veterinarian. Or an engineer. Or a poet. Or whatever he damn well wants to be. A Nobel Peace Prize winner. An Oscar. A Grammy. The poet laureate. I want a happy ending. Or two. I want him to live in the possibility. In his possibility.

And that is why I am here—jailhouse librarian. And that's why I keep coming back.

THE FACTS

No matter which side of the bars you're on, being in prison takes its toll.

- According to the Archives of Suicide Research, the risk of suicide among corrections officers was 39 percent higher than the rest of the working population.

- Suicide rates for the jail population are three times that of the general population.

- In the daily life of a CO, the odds are two to one of being jumped or physically assaulted.[1]

- Heart disease was the leading cause among illness deaths in local jails (42 percent).[2]

- Officers, their families, and inmates are in danger of contracting HIV, hepatitis B and C, tuberculosis and other contagious, and sometimes deadly diseases, at a much higher rate than the general population.[3]

- A CO's fifty-ninth birthday, on average, is his last.[4]

Jail is a dangerous place. For everyone. The United States has about 5 percent of the world's population, but we have 25 percent of the world's prisoners. We incarcerate a greater percentage of our population than any country on Earth.[5]

- The US now incarcerates 500,000 youths per year, more than any other country on the planet.[6]

- The United States spends close to $79 billion a year on keeping the incarcerated in jail.[7]

- In 2010, "The Price of Prisons" estimated that the cost of incarcerating one inmate was $31,307 per year. In places like Connecticut or New York, the cost rose to $50,000 to $60,000.[8] The most recent budget report in New York City estimated its average annual cost per inmate at $167,731.[9]

- According to the Bureau of Labor Statistics, the median annual wage of correctional officers was $39,020 in May 2010.[10]

- In New York City, it costs about $11,844.00 to keep a student in school; right now, it runs about $60,000 to keep them locked up.[11]

Students fail. Students drop out. We fail our students.

- Young high school dropouts are more than sixty-three times more likely to be incarcerated than a high school graduate.[12]

- Studies show that educators can predict high school dropouts as early as sixth grade.[13]

- In the 2009–10 school year, 96,000 students were arrested, and 242,000 referred to law enforcement by schools in what has become known as the "school-to-jail pipeline." [14]

- Black and Hispanic students made up more than 70 percent of the arrested or referred students. [15]

- The most highly represented percentage of students with disabilities in the juvenile justice system are youth with emotional disturbance, 47.4 percent, or learning disabilities, 38.6 percent. [16]

- Recidivism rates average 46 percent for youthful offenders. The typically poor outcomes related to reintegration and recidivism of these youth, with and without disabilities, are estimated to cost society $1.5 million for each person who begins criminal activity as a youth and continues throughout life. [17]

Jail doesn't look good, no matter which side of the bars you are on. Jail isn't the solution for everybody. It isn't the only solution. One million dollars invested in incarceration reduces 350 crimes; one million dollars invested in education reduces 600 crimes. [18]

That's a fact.

"When a book leaves your hands, it belongs to God. He may use it to save a few souls or to try a few others, but I think that for the writer to worry is to take over God's business."
—Flannery O'Connor

RESOURCES

American Library Association. "Helping Libraries Meet The Diverse Needs of Teens Report." 2012. Young Adult Library Services Association. http://www.ala. org/yalsa/sites/ala.org.yalsa/files/content/FinalRpt_ DG2012.pdf.

_____. "Prisoners Re-Entering the Community." American Library Association Office of Literacy & Outreach. http://www.ala.org/offices/sites/ala.org. offices/files/content/olos/prison_reentering.pdf.

_____. "Prisoners' Right to Read." *ALA Intellectual Freedom Manual 8th edition.* June 29, 2010. http:// www.ifmanual.org/prisoners.

_____. "Issue Brief: Teens Need Libraries." Young Adult Library Services Association. http://www.ala.org/ yalsa/sites/ala.org.yalsa/files/content/IssueBrief_ TeensNeedLibrariesx_0.pdf.

Arya, Neelum, Francisco Villarruel, Cassandra Villanueva, and Ian Augarten. "America's Invisible Children: Latino Youth and the Failure of Justice." Policy Brief: Campaign For Youth Justice 3: 95. 2009. http://www.ramseyjdai. org/pdf/readings/latino-invisible-children.pdf.

Austin, Jeanie. "Critical Issues in Juvenile Detention Center Libraries." *The Journal of Research on Libraries and Young Adults 1.* 2012. http://www.yalsa.ala.org/jrlya/2012/07/critical-issues-in-juvenile-detention-center-libraries/.

Bilchik, Shay. "Five Emerging Practices in Juvenile Reentry" *CSG Justice Center for Juvenile Justice Reform Advisory Committee Report.* May 31, 2011. http://csgjusticecenter.org/youth/posts/five-emerging-practices-in-juvenile-reentry/.

Birckhead, Tara. "Shutting Down The School to Prison Pipeline." *Huffington Post.* October 26, 2012. http://www.huffingtonpost.com/tamar-birckhead/stopping-the-school-to-pr_b_2020945.html.

Bouchard, Joe. "5 most dangerous contraband items of 2012." 2012. http://www.correctionsone.com/contraband/articles/4835099-5-most-dangerous-contraband-items-of-2012/.

Bureau of Justice Statistics. "Education and Corrections Report." *NCJ*, 195670: 9. 2003. http://www.bjs.gov/content/pub/pdf/ecp.pdf.

Bureau of Labor Statistics, US Department of Labor, *Occupational Outlook Handbook*, 2012–13 Edition, Correctional Officers. April 26, 2012. http://www.bls.gov/ooh/protective-service/correctional-officers.htm.

California State Department of Corrections and Rehabilitation. "Pelican Bay State Prison." 2013. http://www.cdcr.ca.gov/Facilities_Locator/PBSP.html.

Clark, Cherie, David W. Aziz, and Doris L. MacKenzie. "Shock Incarceration In New York State: Focus on Treatment." *National Institute of Justice Program Focus NCJ 148410:1.* 1994.

Colman, Zack. "Hurricane Sandy Forced Third-Most People from Homes Worldwide in 2012." *E2 Wire: The Hill's Energy & Conservation Blog.* 2012. http://www.thehill.com.

Colorado State Library. "Book Lists: Library Services for Youth in Custody." 2012. http://www.youthlibraries.org/book-lists-all.

Correction Association of New York, The. Juvenile Detention Fact Sheet" *Mayor's Management Report, Fiscal Year 2007.* 2007. www.prisonpolicy.org/scans/detention_fact_2007.pdf.

Correction Association of New York, The. Juvenile Detention Fact Sheet" *Mayor's Management Report, Fiscal Year 2007.* 2007. www.prisonpolicy.org/scans/detention_fact_2007.pdf.

Council of State Governments. "NRRC Facts & Trends." 2013. CSG Justice Center. http://csgjusticecenter.org/nrrc/facts-and-trends/.

Davis, Lois, Robert Bozick, Jennifer Steele, and Jeremy Miles. "Evaluating the Effectiveness of Correctional Education: A Meta-Analysis of Programs That Provide Education to Incarcerated Adults." *RAND Corporation* 6. 2013. http://www.rand.org/pubs/research_reports/RR266.

Davis, Lois. "To Stop Prisons' Revolving Door." RAND Corporation. September 16, 2013. http://www.rand.org/commentary/2013/09/16/LAT.html .

Department of Justice. "US Prison Population Declined For Third Consecutive Year." *Bureau of Justice Statistics.* July 25, 2013. http://www.bjs.gov/content/pub/presee/p12acpr.cfm

Dervan, Lucian, and Vanessa Edkins. "The Innocent Defendant's Dilemma: An Innovative Empirical Study of Plea Bargaining's Innocence Problem." *The Journal of Criminal Law & Criminology,* 103, no. 1. 2013. http://www.law.northwestern.edu/journals/jclc/backissues/v103/n1/1031_1.Dervan.pdf.

Dowling, Brendan. "Public Libraries & Ex-Offenders." *Public Libraries* 46, no. 6. 2007. http://www.ala.org/pla/sites/ala.org.pla/files/content/publications/publiclibraries/pastissues/pl_46n6.pdf.

Education Voters of Pennsylvania. "Saving Futures, Saving Dollars: The Impact of Education on Crime Reduction and Earnings." August 2006. The Alliance for Excellent Education, Washington DC (as quoted in "Education and Crime Issues"). http://www.educationvoterspa.org/index.php/site/issues/education-and-crime/

_____. "Education and Crime Issues." 2010. http://www.educationvoterspa.org/index.php/site/issues/education-and-crime/.

Eldridge, Jamie. "S1134: An Act establishing a special commission on prisoner and correctional officer suicides" January 22, 2013. State Senator Jamie Eldridge Legislative Page. 188th Session Massachusetts State Legislature. http://www.senatoreldridge.com.

Fatherless Generation. "Statistics" *Blog.* 2010. http://thefatherlessgeneration.wordpress.com/statistics/.

Finn, Peter. "Addressing Correctional Officer Stress: Programs & Strategies." *National Institute of Justice Report NCJ 183474.* December 2000. https://www.ncjrs.gov/pdffiles1/nij/183474.pdf.

Fleischer, Matthew. "US Prisons Don't Fund Education, and Everybody Pays a Price." *TakePart.* March 1, 2013. http://www.takepart.com/article/2013/03/01/americas-inmates-education-denied-everybody-pays-price.

Gagnon, J.C., and C. Richards. "Improving Transition Outcomes for Youth Involved in the Juvenile Justice System: Practical Considerations." *National Collaborative on Workforce and Disability/Youth Brief,* Issue 25. March 2010. http://www.ncwd-youth.info/information-brief-25.

Glaze, Lauren, and Laura Maruschak. "Parents in Prison and Their Minor Children." *Bureau of Justice Statistics Special Report. NCJ* 222984. August 2008. http://www.bjs.gov/content/pub/pdf/pptmc.pdf.

Glennor, "Prison Reentry: Dan Rodricks and an Ex-Offender." *Prison Librarian.* September 9, 2012. http://prisonlibrarian.blogspot.com/search/label/Prison%20Reentry.

Guenther, Lisa. "The Living Death of Solitary Confinement." *The New York Times.* Opinionator. August 26, 2012. http://opinionator.blogs.nytimes.com/2012/08/26/the-living-death-of-solitary-confinement/?_r=0.

Higgins, Nick. "A Guide for the Formerly Incarcerated to Information Sources in New York City." *Connections.* Spring 2013. http://www.nypl.org/sites/default/files/12g-221_connections-final2.pdf.

Hogan, Matthew. "Nov. 6: Hurricane Sandy Updates From LIRR, Nassau." *Rockville Centre Patch.* November 6, 2012. http://rockvillecentre.patch.com/groups/politics-and-elections/p/nov-6-hurricane-sandy-updates-from-lirr-nassau.

Human Rights Watch. "US: Number of Mentally Ill in Prisons Quadrupled." *Human Rights Watch News.* September 6, 2006. http://www.hrw.org/news/2006/09/05/us-number-mentally-ill-prisons-quadrupled.

James, Austin, and Michael P. Jacobson. "How New York City Reduced Mass Incarceration." In *Brennan Center for Justice, The JFA Institute & Vera Institute of Justice Policy Report* 1:26. January 30, 2013. http://www.brennancenter.org/publication/how-new-york-city-reduced-mass-incarceration-model-change.

Justice Center: The Council of State Governments. "NRRC Facts & Trends." 2013. http://csgjusticecenter.org/nrrc/facts-and-trends/.

Kennelly, Louise, and Maggie Monrad. "Approaches to Dropout Prevention: Heeding the Early Warning Signs With Appropriate Interventions." *National High School Center.* October 2007. www.betterhighschools.org/docs/nhsc_approachestodropoutprevention.pdf.

Kerby, Sofia. "10 Most Startling Facts About People of Color and the Criminal Justice System in America." (In "Issues: Race & Ethnicity. Center for American Progress.") March 13, 2012. http://www.americanprogress.org/issues/race/news/2012/03/13/11351/the-top-10-most-startling-facts-about-people-of-color-and-criminal-justice-in-the-united-states/.

Knewton, *Breaking the Prison Cycle through Education.* Infographic. Houghton Mifflin Company, Inc. 2013. http://www.knewton.com/prison-education/.

Kysell, Ian. "Ban solitary confinement for youth in care of the federal government." *Human Rights Watch News.* April 11, 2013. http://www.hrw.org/

news/2013/04/11/ban-solitary-confinement-youth-care-federal-government.

Latino Justice. "Nassau County Police Department to Strengthen Language Access Services." LatinoJustice: 2013. http://latinojustice.org/briefing_room/press_releases/NASSAU_COUNTY_POLICE_DEPARTMENT_TO_STRENGTHEN_LANGUAGE_ACCESS_SERVICES/.

Leaming, Jeremy. "Ineffective Indigent Defense System Fuels Mass Incarceration, Brennan Center Report Says." *American Constitution Society for Law and Policy Blog.* April 9, 2013. www.acslaw.or/acsblog/ineffective-indigent-defense-system-fuels-mass-incarceration-brennan-center-report-says.

Levin, Henry M., and William H. Kilpatrick, comps. *The Social Costs of Inadequate Education.* Publication. Campaign for Educational Equity, 2005. Teachers College Symposium on Educational Equity. Teachers College, Columbia University, 24–26 October 2005 (Web March 2010).

Lilienthal, Stephen. "Prison and Libraries: Public Service Inside and Out." *Library Journal,* February 4, 2013. http://lj.libraryjournal.com/2013/02/library-services/prison-and-public-libraries/.

Limited English Proficiency (LEP) "Frequently Asked Questions (FAQs)." http://www.lep.gov/faqs/faqs.html#OneQ11.

Lindquist, Rusty. "I am the master of my fate, the captain of my soul, Invictus." *Life-Engineering.* December 19, 2010. http://life-engineering.com/1935/i-am-the-master-of-my-fate-invictus/.

Liptak, Adam. "Supreme Court to Weigh Effects of Bad Plea Advice." *The New York Times*. October 30, 2011. http://www.nytimes.com/2011/10/31/us/supreme-court-to-hear-cases-involving-bad-advice-on-plea-deals.html?_r=0.

Mendocino County, "Inmate Nutrition." *Medicino County Grand Jury Report 1*. May 1, 2013. http://www.co.mendocino.ca.us/grandjury/pdf/1213 InmateNutrition.pdf.

Naim, Cyrus. "Prison Food Law." Spring 2005. LEDA at Harvard Law School. http://dash.harvard.edu/bitstream/handle/1/8848245/Naim05.html?sequence=2.

National Association For The Advancement of Colored People. "Criminal Justice Fact Sheet." 2009–13. https://donate.naacp.org/pages/criminal-justice-fact-sheet.

National Gang Intelligence Center. "2011 National Gang Threat Assessment: Emerging Trends." 1: 11. 2011.

National Institute of Corrections. "Correctional Officer Life Expectancy." *NIC Information Center*. June 11, 2010. https://nic.zendesk.com/entries/192542-Correctional-Officer-Life-Expectancy.

National Institute of Justice. "US Prison Population Declined For Third Consecutive Year." *Bureau of Justice Statistics Report*. NCJ 242467. July 25, 2013. http://www.bjs.gov/content/pub/presee/p12acpr.cfm.

New York Public Library. "NYPL Correctional Services Fact Sheet." 2012. http://www.nypl.org.

New York State Department of Corrections and Community Supervision. "Who is Eligible for A Certificate of

Relief?" 2013. https://www.parole.ny.gov/certrelief.html.

New York State Department of Education. "Education of Incarcerated Youth Program Plan Review Guide: Alternative and Incarcerated Education: P-12." 2010. http://www.p12.nysed.gov/sss/ssae/AltEd/reviewguide.html.

New York State Juvenile Justice Advisory Group. "Tough On Crime: Promoting Public Safety by Doing What Works." December 2010. http://criminaljustice.state.ny.us/pio/annualreport/2010-juvenile-justice-annual-report.pdf.

New York State Unified Court System. "Candidate Guide to the Language Assessment Testing Program for Court Interpreting." 2010. http://www.nycourts.gov/courtinterpreter/pdfs/candidateguide.pdf.

Noonan, Margaret. "Deaths in Custody Reporting Program Mortality in Local Jails, 2000–2007." *Bureau of Special Statistics Special Report.* Washington, DC: US Department of Justice. *NCJ* 222988. July 2010.

Nutall, John, Linda Hollemen, and Michelle Staley. "The Effect of Earning a GED on Recidivism Rates." *Journal of Correctional Education* 1. 2003. http://www.passged.com/media/pdf/research/The_Effect_of_Earning_a_GED_on_Recidivisim_Rates.pdf.

Palta, Rina. "Researchers Say Plea Bargains Actually Send Innocent Defendants To Jail." *The Latest.* June 13, 2012. Southern California Public Radio. KPCC. https://www.google.com/#fp=ece303f9a3bf8e22&q=researchers+say+plea+bargains+actually+send+innocent+defendants+to+jail.

Parker, Scott, Kamilla Mallik-Kane, and Aaron Horvath. "Opportunities for Information Sharing to Enhance Health and Public Safety Outcomes." September 5, 2013. The Urban Institute. http://www.urban.org/justice/corrections.cfm.

Prison Studies Project: Teaching, Research and Outreach. "Why Prison Education?" 2011. http://prisonstudiesproject.org/why-prison-education-programs/.

Public Servants Rule. "Corrections Officers and the Dangers They Face." *Public Servants Rule.* February 8, 2009. http://www.publicservantsrule.com/blog/2009/02/08/corrections-officers-and-the-dangers-they-face.html.

Ranganathan, S. R. *The Five Laws of Library Science.* 1931. HathiTrust Digital Library. http://hdl.handle.net/2027/uc1.b99721.

Rhonda, S., A. A. Reichard and H. M. Tiesman. "Occupational injuries among US correctional officers, 1999–2008." 2012. *J Safety Res.* PubMed/NIH. National Center for Biotechnology Information. http://www.ncbi.nlm.nih.gov/pubmed/22974683.

Rosenberg, Tina. "Out of Jail and Into A Job." *The New York Times.* March 28, 2012. http://opinionator.blogs.nytimes.com/2012/03/28/out-of-jail-and-into-jobs/.

Santora, Frank. "City's Annual Cost Per Inmate Is $168,000, Study Finds." *The New York Times.* August 24, 2013. http://www.nytimes.com/2013/08/24/nyregion/citys-annual-cost-per-inmate-is-nearly-168000-study-says.html.

Shiffman, Lizzie, "Preckwinkle: A Harvard Education Is Cheaper Than Jailing Youth." *Huffington Post:*

Chicago. October 21, 2011. http://www.huffington
post.com/2011/10/21/preckwinkle-details-budge_n_
1023833.html.

State Library of Iowa. "The Steps of the Reference
Interview." 2013. http://www.statelibraryofiowa.org/
ld/i-j/infolit/toolkit/geninfo/refinterview.

Steele, Donald. "Stress Management for the Professional
Correctional Officer." *Corrections Yearbook 2000,
2002.* Criminal Justice Institute. Middletown, Ct:
Steele Publishing. 2001.

Stengel, Richard, "Sharing Mandela's Way In Fifteen
Lessons." *Talk of the Nation.* NPR Radio. April 10, 2010.
Interview hosted by Neal Conan. http://www.npr.
org/templates/story/story.php?storyId=126136918

Sum, Andrew, Ishwar Khatiwada, and Joseph McLaughlin.
"The Consequences of Dropping Out of High
School Joblessness and Jailing for High School
Dropouts and the High Cost for Taxpayers."
Center for Labor Studies. Boston: Northeastern
University, October 2009. http://iris.lib.neu.edu/cgi/
viewcontent.cgi?article=1022&context=clms_pub.

Teichner, Marsha. "The Cost of a Nation of Incarceration."
CBS Sunday Morning. April 22, 2012.

Thomas Reuters. "Plea Bargains In Depth." 2013. http://
criminal.findlaw.com/criminal-procedure/plea-
bargains-in-depth.html.

TorsBijns, Carl. "Stress, the Correctional Officer's Silent
Killer." December 17, 2012. http://www.corrections.
com/articles/31896.

United States Department of Justice. "Prison Gangs." 2013.
http://www.justice.gov/criminal/ocgs/gangs/prison.html.

United States Department of Labor. "Nonfatal Occupational Injuries and Illnesses Requiring Days Away From Work, 2011." November 8, 2012. US Bureau of Labor Statistics Economic News Release USDL-12-2204. http://www.bls.gov/news.release/osh2.nr0.htm.

University of the State of New York. "Frequently Asked Questions (FAQ)." Adult Career and Continuing Education Services. October 17, 2013. http://www.acces.nysed.gov/ged/faq_answers.html.

US Department of Education. "Fast Facts: Dropout Rates." National Center for Education Statistics. 2013. http://nces.ed.gov/fastfacts/display.asp?id=16.

US Department of Health & Human Services. "Parents' Tips: Calories Needed Each Day." *We Can! Ways to Enhance Children's Nutrition & Activity Newsletter.* 2010. http://www.nhlbi.nih.gov/health/public/heart/obesity/wecan/downloads/calreqtips.pdf.

US Department of Labor. *Correctional Officers: Occupational Outlook Handbook : US Bureau of Labor Statistics.* April 26, 2012. http://www.bls.gov/ooh/protective-service/correctional-officers.htm#tab-1.

Vera Institute of Justice. "The Price of Prison: What Incarceration Costs Taxpayers (New York) Fact Sheet." January 26, 2012. Vera Institute of Justice 1:53. http://www.vera.org/news/new-vera-report-price-prisons-what-incarceration-costs-taxpayers.

Veronese, Keith. "10 Revolting Foods That People Make in Prison." July 30, 2012. *io9: We Come From The Future.* http://io9.com/5930053/10-revolting-foods-that-people-have-made-in-prison.

Wikipedia. "Five laws of library science." October 6, 2013. http://en.wikipedia.org/wiki/Five_laws_of_library_science#Variants.

_____. "New Mexico State Penitentiary riot." October 21, 2013. http://en.wikipedia.org/wiki/New_Mexico_State_Penitentiary_riot.

_____. "Rastafari Movement." http://en.wikipedia.org/wiki/Rastafari_movement.

Wolf-Harlow, Caroline. "Defense Counsel in Criminal Cases." Bureau of Justice Statistics Special Report 179023. 2000. http://www.bjs.gov/content/pub/pdf/dccc.pdf.

Young, Douglas, Rachel Porter, and Gail A. Caputo. "Alternative to Incarceration Programs for Felony Offenders In New York City." Vera Institute of Justice Report 1, no. 364.6 YD: 2. 1999.

ACKNOWLEDGMENTS

There are not enough thanks for the many who have inspired me, helped me, given me a read through, or checked a misspelled word or two. Without them, I'd still be sitting in a Brooklyn coffee shop with a blank computer screen. First and foremost, my mother and father. For my late husband, John, whose last journal urged me to find my voice. For my husband Michael, who helped me find it. For my three children, Margaret, John, and Paul. For my daughter-in-law, Gretchen Gonzalez, Uncle Charles. For my editors, Kathy Jefferies, Elizabeth Skolnick, Mary Ann Brendler, Mike Riordan, Donna Brennan, Dottie Brandreth. For my "editor-niece," Colleen McCormick. A great editor, Marly Cornell. And Allison. Pat Benjamin, CSW. The Laura Bush Scholarship Foundation. St. John's University School of Library Science. METRO New York Library Council Prison Librarian's Group. For my mentor, Sheila Rule, one of the best editors and a strong advocate and voice for the incarcerated. *Think Outside The Cell*—which led me to think outside of mine. For Sister Dolores Castellano, CIJ, who inspires me through all of her ministries, and who is now not only my friend but also my editor. The NCCC Prison Ministry. For Wayne Ament, who kept telling me that I should write a book. A great boss, Scott Woerner. East Meadow Schools. For John Marciante and all those other teachers who support the boys here in jail. Nassau County Sheriff's Correction Officers Benevolent Association. For Jerry Nichols, one of the most versatile librarians around, and his lovely wife, Mary, both of whom encouraged my telling this librarian's story. Mary Robinson, Renee McGrath, and Elizabeth Olesh at the Nassau County Library System. For Margaret Dennis, my forever Brooklyn bud, and her son Will Dennis at DC Comics. For John Gallagher, thank you for your comments and your friendship. For my cheerleaders, Anne C., Paula, Betty, Anne B., Mary, Jeanne, Byron, Dawn, Bob, Anne O., Darlene, Julian, Justin, Joanne, Joyce, all Women In The Spirit—who "loved me until I could love myself." For the writers who've inspired my life and who've surrounded me, especially Arelis, Ellie, and David. For my coworkers, Sue, Holly, Jon, Richie, Ken, Moe, Bob, Richie, Michele, Sahed, Carmine, Sandy, Milton, Roman, Evans and Johnson, I know there must be a fine for writing this—I'll pay up at the next kangaroo court. Muchas gracias, Ivan. Grateful to these kind readers, Nick Higgins, Donna Rosenblum, Amy Cheney and Elizabeth Marshak. For the patience, steady hand and red pen of Bob Keeler. For the generosity of the World Book Night Foundation. A subway miracle, Adrian. Blessings, Meryl, Rachel and Jon. For all of the workers at Panera Bread in East Meadow ... great coffee and Wi-Fi.

ABOUT THE AUTHOR

Marybeth Zeman has been a teacher on the elementary, high school, and college level for more than thirty years and, since 2010, has served as transitional counselor for a school program for incarcerated youth in a large suburban county jail.

In 2009 she was awarded a Laura Bush 21st Century Librarian Scholarship from St. John's University, where she earned a master's degree in Library Science and Information Services. She thought she was adding credentials to her resume. Little did she realize that she would be creating a jail library.

A lifelong New Yorker, Marybeth lives in Fort Greene, Brooklyn, with her husband Michael and two cats, Delhia and Susie.

ENDNOTES

The Facts

1 Steele.

2 Noonan.

3 *Public Servants Rule.*

4 Steele.

5 Kerby.

6 Knewton.

7 Ibid.

8 Ibid.

9 Santora.

10 Bureau of Labor Statistics.

11 The Correction Association of New York.

12 Teichner.

13 Kennelly and Monrad.

14 Sum, et al.

15 Kerby.

16 Gagnon.

17 Ibid.

18 Knewton.

23918904R00194

Made in the USA
Middletown, DE
07 September 2015